Student Data Privacy

Student Data Privacy

Building a School Compliance Program

Linnette Attai

ROWMAN & LITTLEFIELD
Lanham • Boulder • New York • London

Published by Rowman & Littlefield
A wholly owned subsidiary of The Rowman & Littlefield Publishing Group, Inc.
4501 Forbes Boulevard, Suite 200, Lanham, Maryland 20706
www.rowman.com

Unit A, Whitacre Mews, 26-34 Stannary Street, London SE11 4AB

British Library Cataloguing in Publication Information Available

Library of Congress Cataloging-in-Publication Data Is Available

ISBN 978-1-4758-3735-3 (cloth : alk. paper)
ISBN 978-1-4758-3736-0 (pbk. : alk. paper)
ISBN 978-1-4758-3737-7 (electronic)

∞™ The paper used in this publication meets the minimum requirements of American
National Standard for Information Sciences—Permanence of Paper for Printed Library
Materials, ANSI/NISO Z39.48-1992.

Printed in the United States of America

Parents trust that school systems will care for the safety of their children. Today, that fundamental responsibility of care must extend to protecting the privacy of students' personal information.

For those who know what it's going to take, and do it anyway.

Contents

Introduction

Today's school systems contain a rich mixture of technology to facilitate student education and classroom management. With that comes the collection of data from and about students, used in a variety of ways to fulfill the purpose of education, described by Arthur W. Foshay as "to bring people as full a realization as possible of what it is to be a human being."[1]

It's a suitably broad and lofty description, encompassing a responsibility to impart knowledge, develop intellect and character, foster readiness and aptitude for college and career, protect students from harm, and properly manage the ecosystem in which that work happens.

The technology used to support that purpose is diverse, as is the data collected and the stakeholders involved. It encompasses all of following and more:

- names, addresses, student IDs, and sometimes Social Security numbers, parent names, and custodial arrangements;
- classroom performance and behavior, grades, and attendance;
- height, weight, physical abilities, and limitations;
- allergies, medications, and injuries ranging from everyday scrapes and bruises to the impacts of abuse;
- behavioral information;
- learning preferences and aptitudes;
- future goals and learning plans;
- disabilities and accommodations;

- financial information and free and reduced lunch qualification; and
- bus schedules and other transportation arrangements.

Much of this data—whether collected via technology or not—has been gathered by schools for generations. As a society, there was general acceptance that schools were repositories of vast amounts of student information. In the 1970s, federal student data privacy laws in the form of the Family Educational Rights and Privacy Act (FERPA) and the Protection of Pupil Rights Amendment (PPRA) provided requirements for school systems about how to properly manage the privacy of that data. For a time after that, there seemed to be a quiet satisfaction, or at least acceptance, about the amount of information collected by schools. There was certainly little scrutiny over how schools actually protected the data.

With the technology-enabled classroom came even more data collection. It is now possible to know not just who a student is, but what machine the student is using, at what time, for how long, what website pages are clicked, whether or not the student is engaged in a lesson, what happens after viewing a lesson, and more. Many times, that information is collected in a manner that does not intentionally identify the student, but instead is analyzed in the aggregate, across all students to better understand how they interact with a product, and where and how a product may be improved.

However, it is often possible to connect the information in such a way that identifies an individual, and to use the data in more ways than ever before. It is also now possible to understand not just how a student learns but to follow the student's interaction with instructional materials so closely that we can know exactly when the student's attention drops off, where the student moves through the material with ease, or where the student begins to struggle.

There are tremendous benefits to this. It's easier to create individualized learning plans when we can rely on machines to analyze the data. Lessons can be adjusted, tailored, and customized, sometimes in the moment, to benefit the individual student. We can better manage and support diverse classroom environments, in which each student is able to learn in their own way, at their own pace. We can more accurately identify which students are at risk, and what interventions are most effective at supporting those students to help them stay on track with their education.

However, these advances have also come with questions and a good deal of fear: fear of where the data might go and who might have access, fear of technology providers, fear of the old laws being inadequate to meet the privacy challenges of new technologies, fear of screen time, and fear of change.

Too often, school systems have been ill-equipped to provide parents with the information they need about how and why data is collected, used, and protected to allow parents to make fact-based judgments about their child's work in a classroom that no longer resembles the one of their youth.[2]

Significant areas of concern have been reflected in questions from parents, legislators, and other interested community members. They can be summarized into two key areas:

1. When school systems are collecting more data than ever before from and about their students, how can parents, students, and other community stakeholders be assured that the school system needs that information and is managing and protecting the data properly, in accordance with the legal requirements, district rules, and community norms?
2. As school systems rely on technology providers to manage collection, storage, and handling of student data, how can parents, students, and other community stakeholders be assured that the school systems are maintaining control over the student data and how it is used by technology providers?

The short answer to both of these questions is "governance" or, more specifically, "compliance." A program of operations and rules of behavior, codified in measurable, auditable policies and practices, creates the framework for ensuring a school system meets its legal and ethical obligations to protect student data privacy and can provide parents and students with the evidence to demonstrate that the program operates as designed.

Building a data compliance program is no small endeavor. This book focuses on the area of compliance concerned with protecting the privacy of student personal information. That corner of compliance is a significant and critical undertaking. It also requires a lasting commitment to the work. A student data privacy compliance program is a living, breathing, ever-evolving function that, in the case of school systems, expands and modernizes the existing ethos of school system responsibility the twenty-first century classroom.

It is with this in mind, and a focus on the responsibility inherent in working with students, upon which we build the foundations of a data privacy compliance program.

AUTHOR NOTE

In these pages, "school system" refers to an educational agency or institution of any organizational or governance structure. In addition, while the laws use very different terminology to define information that could be used to identify a student, it's been simplified here to refer simply to "student personal information," except when the discussion is centered on a specific law, in which case, the legally defined term is used.

References to "parent" are intended to be inclusive of the legal guardian, and "technology provider" refers to any vendor, contractor, operator, or similar individual or organization providing technology products, including websites, apps, and other Internet-connected products and services to a school system.

Please note that this book does not cover every scenario in which student data privacy might be impacted, as that would take volumes. It does, however, provide a framework that can then be applied to all facets of student data privacy across school system operations.

Finally, please also note that this is not, and should not be construed as legal or professional advice of any kind. It is also not all-inclusive. It is my observations, based on my nearly thirty years as a compliance practitioner, working with organizations ranging from small and large schools and districts, education technology companies of all sizes, global gaming companies, and entertainment media conglomerates in the United States and abroad. It eschews complex rubrics and related tools often used to frame out and audit such programs. Instead, it is meant to be a realistic, accessible, simple, and straightforward look at how to consider and begin to build a data privacy compliance program.

If you have not yet begun to build your school system's data privacy compliance program, the prospect may, at time, seem overwhelming. There is a wealth of detail to consider. However, take heart in knowing that you are not alone in the journey. It is a long road, but every small step you take is progress. Let's begin.

Chapter 1

What Is Data Privacy Compliance?

Data governance refers to the overall organizational management of the availability, integrity, protection, and usability of data in an organization. It includes leadership to oversee and steer the program, and it incorporates a collection of policies that articulate expectations and procedures to bring those expectations to fruition. In short, data governance is about the authority over and decisions made about data.[1]

It covers the entire lifecycle of data, from collection to destruction. It incorporates an organizational structure clarifying who has the authority for what decisions; requirements for collecting, handling, using, disclosing, and deleting data; ensuring the security and integrity of the data; enforceable policies and procedures to implement the governance program; a program to monitor compliance; auditing of the program; and transparency about the program.

Compliance, often used informally and interchangeably with governance, is actually a subset of governance. It is how the organization aligns with the requirements to protect personal information. As a function, data privacy compliance is concerned with establishing, implementing, and enforcing the portion of an organization's data governance program related to protecting the privacy of personal information.

When done well, a school system data privacy compliance program is not about restriction. It's about empowering individuals and teams to make smart, consistent, auditable decisions about data use that benefit the students they serve. It allows for ethical use of data to support student success, make better decisions, allow for more efficient operations, mitigate risk, and maintain control over the data throughout its lifecycle.

WHAT IS DATA PRIVACY ALL ABOUT?

One last term to understand is "data privacy." On the surface, it may seem obvious, but data privacy means different things to different people.

Parents may think of student data privacy to mean the security of their child's data, that is, assurance that bad actors will not hack into a data server and steal their child's information. That theft, or to put it in more neutral terms used in many data breach laws, that "unauthorized access to data," is only part of the picture. Depending on the cause of the unauthorized access, that work may actually sit more appropriately in the discipline of data security.

Privacy and security are related but distinct disciplines. Security deals with maintaining the confidentiality, integrity, and availability of the data. It is a discipline that, while dependent on behavior, also often relies heavily on technology taking the lead in supporting the protection of data. There are a variety of technological tools available and necessary to help ensure the security of information, the servers it is stored in, and the networks it flows through. Firewalls, secure coding practices, multifactor authentication, patching, and virus-scanning are just some of the elements at our disposal that, when implemented properly, help protect the security of the data. Security also encompasses physical protections, including locks on doors, and administrative tools, such as rules about password complexity and policies about who may access what data, that are then often enforced with the help of technology.

For many parents, a lock on the door of data—literally and figuratively—would be a comfort. If only it were that simple.

Young people, on the other hand, are more likely to think of privacy as meaning "personal." For example, a young teen may connect with a parent on a social media platform and keep all of his activity on that site open to his parent. However, if the teen is engaged in a conversation on social media with friends, he may find it intrusive if the parent chimes in on the discussion. To young people, those discussions are meant to be "private." For many young people, managing privacy is a complex process of controlling when, where, and how they share personal information and how it will be received. In that sense, the definition of privacy takes shape in accordance with context.[2]

Although it may not seem clear at first glance, the young person's view of privacy actually has some relation to the modern-day privacy norms, in that it considers who may have access to what information, and how privacy is ensured may depend on the sensitivity of the data and the context in which it is being shared and used. While this does not encompass all aspects of data privacy, it does touch on an important point, which is that not everyone is permitted access to all information.

Privacy can be broadly defined as the right to determine for ourselves when, how, and what information we communicate to others. Privacy is important, in part, because how we view it is personal.

For our purposes, in discussing how a school system protects the privacy of student personal information, we'll refer to it simply as a discipline concerned with what data we gather and how we handle it.

The discipline of data privacy is implemented via a broad range of policies, processes, and practices that govern what information we collect, why we collect it, what we do with it, how and to whom it is disclosed, and when it is deleted. What those rules are depends, at a minimum, on the regulations. However, when developed properly, the rules are elevated to encompass not only the baseline standards of legal compliance, but the school system's mission and vision, its ethical boundaries, and the expectations of the community in which the school system operates.

Privacy is a discipline of behavior. It does not require vast expenditures on complex infrastructures, although certainly there are technologies that are often necessary, or at least helpful, in supporting a privacy program. It does require individuals with specific expertise, as well as rules and norms in the form of enforceable policies and processes. Technology can support privacy efforts, but it is our behavior that makes privacy efforts successful.

As related disciplines, privacy and security go hand-in-hand. All of the security protections you can implement are not sufficient to protect the data without a robust privacy program, and privacy alone is also insufficient—it requires a strong security framework to address what behavior alone cannot.

Chapter 2

How Did We Get Here?

When did school systems first need to be concerned with data privacy? The answer is really "when school systems were first built," but of course, the climate of fear around data privacy came well after that. Even the introduction of classroom technologies did not spark the questions and fears that exist today.

Instead, as far as recent history goes, we can mark 2013 as the year that parents, parent advocates, and legislators realized that classrooms had changed so much as to be almost wholly unfamiliar, and that technology used in the classroom could have implications for the privacy of student personal information. They raised meaningful and important questions about how student personal information was being protected, and many school systems, government agencies, and technology providers at the time were not prepared with good answers.

The climate of fear was sparked in part by a variety of events that happened in a very short time span. It was almost inevitable that things would change as a result.

It started with the famous, or infamous, story of inBloom, the technology initiative that promised to increase the possibilities and potential for personalized learning but failed to clearly articulate not only the benefits of the technology but also how student data would be properly protected.[1] It was a massive, swift, and very public rise and fall.

Around that same time, the country was grappling with the Edward Snowden revelations about government surveillance of personal information, as well as the massive Target data breach.

Often forgotten, however, was the additional scrutiny at the time that was focused specifically on school systems and how they protect the privacy of student personal information when working with technology providers. The *New York Times* published an article by Natasha Singer discussing inBloom, accompanied by a rather alarming graphic in the form of a silhouette of a person illustrated as multiple data points, with the caption, "You for Sale."[2] The article contained a quote that stated unequivocally, "there are too few safeguards for the amount of data collected and transmitted from schools to private companies."[3]

Less than three weeks later, Senator Edward Markey (D-MA) sent a letter to the then US Department of Education Secretary Arne Duncan, citing the article in the *New York Times* and noting that it raised questions about how student data might be used by technology companies and "the degree to which student data might be compromised."[4] Senator Markey continued by asking rather pointed questions about whether or not the Department of Education had fully considered the impact of the 2008 and 2011 changes to the Family Educational Rights and Privacy Act (FERPA) on the privacy of student data.

Senator Markey requested a response within three weeks. Almost twelve weeks later, Secretary Duncan responded.[5] Approximately six months later, Senator Markey introduced the "Protecting Student Data Privacy Act of 2014," a federal bill proposing updates to FERPA.

In the meantime, the Fordham Center for Law and Information Policy released a report titled, "Privacy and Cloud Computing in Public Schools."[6] The report showcased results of an assessment of how school systems managed their legal obligations for protecting student data privacy when working with cloud computing service providers.

It painted a rather scathing picture of school system management over business arrangements with technology providers, detailing a variety of missteps on the part of school systems. These included acceptance by school systems of contracts in which control over the student data was not clearly articulated, and in which technology providers gave what amounted to meaningless assurances that they would "not cause the district to fall out of compliance with FERPA."

The authors cited this as evidence that many school systems simply didn't seem to understand their data privacy and security responsibilities.[7]

It was, indeed, a busy year for student data privacy, fraught with revelations and questions, with no easy answers. What followed was a variety of advocacy and legislative activity across the states in what often seemed like frantic attempts to identify and plug real and imagined holes in the existing regulatory framework. It had a dramatic impact on the awareness among legislators, advocates, parents, school systems, and technology providers about the roles and responsibilities required in order to work productively and successfully with technology in education.

Although there was still a good deal of confusion about how to properly protect student personal information in the face of new technologies, it was clear that answers were needed quickly. It was also clear that for most school systems, those answers could only be found by building a student data privacy compliance program.

Chapter 3

Why Build a Data Privacy Compliance Program?

Establishing a data privacy compliance program is essential to any organization.

It's a complex endeavor focused on establishing the ways in which the organization will and won't manage and use data in alignment with the laws, organizational imperatives, and community norms, then ensuring that everyone in the organization works effectively within those boundaries. This is no small project, and it is not a "one and done" activity. This is about embarking on a holistic program of continuous, everlasting, and ongoing improvement to protect the privacy of individuals whose data has been collected.

It's about identifying and owning the gaps in an existing data protection program and correcting and adjusting to mitigate risk, even as the environment around it and the data flowing through it continue to evolve. It involves education, training, and continuous assessment.

If that all sounds like a moving target, it is. It is also an undertaking that will reach into every corner of the organization.

When done well, the benefits are significant and tangible. Risk is reduced, predictability of practices and efficiency improves, and knowledge and collaboration among teams increases. Within a school system, that often translates to empowering individuals and teams to make smart, consistent, appropriate decisions about data use that benefit the students and parents they collectively support.

It can infuse the organization with a defined purpose for having and using data in the first place. That is because a data privacy compliance program is not just about what can't be done but about invigorating around what can be done, ethically, to support students. To that end, creating a data privacy compliance program often begins by defining the purpose for collecting, using, and sharing data in the first place.

There is a vast range of readiness when it comes to building a data privacy compliance program. It may be that your school system has only small improvements to make in order to increase the maturity of your existing data privacy compliance program, or you may find that your entire organizational culture needs to change in order to create a strong data-protection culture. Most often, the status is somewhere in between.

Regardless of the starting point, implementing a new function is never easy, but it can be made more palatable by first establishing the necessity for the change. In other words, before embarking on such a complex program, it helps to understand why it's important.

THE LAWS

A data privacy compliance program is, in part, the way in which an organization manages its operations in accordance with federal and state privacy regulations. There is simply no way around it. The laws are complex, and consideration for how personal information may and may not be collected, used, and disclosed requires careful planning and controls. Without policies and processes in place to govern employee behavior, there is no accountability against which to measure alignment with the regulatory requirements. It becomes a near-impossible task to ensure that one is following the laws or to demonstrate compliance with the laws.

While this is not intended to be a primer on the laws, it can be helpful to begin by reviewing some of the fundamentals of certain key regulations.

FAMILY EDUCATIONAL RIGHTS AND PRIVACY ACT (FERPA)[1]

FERPA could probably best be referred to as the granddaddy of student data privacy laws. Passed in 1974, but updated via guidances issued in 2008 and

2011, FERPA is enforced by the United States Department of Education (ED) Family Policy Compliance Office (FPCO) and applies to all education institutions that receive federal funding. FERPA affords parents—inclusive of legal guardians—and students who have reached the age of eighteen or who have matriculated at a higher education institution ("eligible students") rights to

- review and inspect the student's education record;
- request that the education institution amend or correct information in the student's education record that the parent or eligible student believes to be inaccurate, misleading, or otherwise in violation of the student's privacy rights;
- a hearing in the event that a request to amend or correct information in the student's record is denied; and
- permit release of personally identifiable information in the student's education record only with prior, signed and dated written consent, except in certain limited circumstances.

Education institutions must notify parents and eligible students each year of their rights under FERPA, along with information about how to exercise those rights. The notice must also be "effectively provided" for the disabled and, in the case of elementary and secondary institutions, to parents whose primary home language is not English.

Education institutions must obtain written consent from the parent or eligible student before releasing personally identifiable information from the education record, except in certain situations. Those circumstances include disclosure to a number of entities, including

- another school to which a student is transferring;
- certain officials for audit or evaluation purposes;
- appropriate parties in connection with determining eligibility in response to a financial aid application;
- organizations conducting certain studies for or on behalf of the school to develop, validate, or administer predictive tests or student aid programs, or to improve instruction;
- accrediting organizations;
- authorized parties in a court case when necessary to comply with a judicial order or lawful subpoena;
- appropriate officials in the case of health and safety emergencies; and
- state and local authorities within a juvenile justice system, in accordance with state law.

Some of these use cases are also restricted by additional conditions that must be met prior to releasing the data.

In addition, the following commonly used exceptions to obtaining prior written consent from the parent or eligible student for the release of student personally identifiable information also apply.

Directory Information

Education institutions may designate certain information about a student to be directory information. Directory information is information that is not considered to be harmful or an invasion of privacy if released. It may—but does not have to—include a student name, address, telephone number, email address, photo, date and place of birth, major field of study, grade level, enrollment status, dates of attendance, participation in officially recognized activities and sports, weight and height of members of athletic teams, degrees, honors and awards, and the most recent educational agency or institution attended.

It may not include a student's Social Security number. It may include a student ID or other unique personal identifier used to access or communicate in electronic systems or displayed on a student ID, only when that identifier cannot be used to access education records except in conjunction with another authentication factor, such as a password or PIN.

Each year, the education institution must provide parents and eligible students with a notice containing the types of personally identifiable information that have been designated as directory information, provide the individual with the opportunity to opt out of having some or all of those types of information designated as directory information (and thus shared under the directory information exception without prior consent), and the deadline for notifying the education institution of the desire to opt out.

This exception for sharing information without prior written consent was intended to allow education institutions to go about their routine business operations and to engage in traditional school activities such as publishing a yearbook, the list of students on the school sports teams, or a program for a school play without having to obtain prior written consent for each activity. This information sharing exception does not include any provisions for maintaining control over the information once it has been shared, which is one of the reasons why it was not intended for use when sharing personally identifiable information from education records with technology providers.

School Officials

When sharing personally identifiable information from education records with technology providers, it's often more appropriate to designate the technology operator as a school official, if the technology provider qualifies as such. School officials are employees, consultants, vendors, volunteers, and other parties that have a legitimate educational interest in receiving student personally identifiable information from education records. In the case of outside parties, to be considered a school official, the party must perform a function for which the education institution would otherwise use its employees.

Under this exception, the education institution must define and inform parents about what constitutes a legitimate educational interest and inform parents and eligible students each year about how it considers and qualifies outside parties to be school officials.

In addition, the education institution must maintain "direct control" over such school officials with respect to their use and maintenance of the personally identifiable information from the education records. This direct control is most often expressed in a contractual agreement between the education institution and the school official. Elements of direct control expressed in contracts include provisions documenting what data will be disclosed, what the data may be used for, how long and under what conditions it may be maintained, when it must be deleted, if it must be returned before being deleted, and how the education institution may access, amend, and correct the information for their purposes or to respond to requests from parents and eligible students wishing to exercise their rights under FERPA.

Establishing "Direct Control"

Direct control means that what the school system says happens with the personally identifiable information from education records goes.

A school system establishing direct control over how a technology provider uses and maintains the data is similar to how a company manages its employees' conduct: policies and procedures set expectations for behavior, and people (or in the case of technology providers, entities) are held accountable for compliance.

(continued)

Expectations for behavior of technology provider might include

- a statement of FERPA restrictions ensuring that personal information from education records
    - may only be used to serve the school system purpose,
    - may not be used or disclosed for any other purpose without prior written consent of the parent or eligible student, and
    - remains under the direct control of the school system;
- physical, technical, and administrative security controls will be put in place to protect the personal information;
- data will be made available in response to requests parents or eligible students to review their education records;
- personal information will be deleted and/or returned at the time agreed upon; and
- contract changes require mutual, written consent.

Control is usually established with a contract. Whether it's a click-wrap agreement or a signed document, the contract establishes legally binding requirements for behavior. It should include provisions that specify what the school system requires of technology providers in terms of how the data may be used and handled, and what happens to the data when the contract ends, all in the manner that the technology provider can and does implement. It should also be clear that the agreement, and thus the school system control over the student personally identifiable information, may not change without mutual, written consent.

Finally, education institutions must ensure that school officials obtain access to only those education records in which they have a legitimate educational interest, and must have physical or technological access controls, or an administrative policy controlling access to the education records, in alignment with the legitimate educational interest requirement.

The school official, in turn, must use the student personal information from education records only to serve the legitimate educational purpose, unless they obtain prior written consent from the parent or eligible student, where such an exception is permitted by the education institution and state law.

Deidentified Data

Information from education records may be disclosed without prior consent from the parent or eligible student if the information has been properly deidentified before being shared.

Sounds simple enough, but deidentification can be a complex undertaking, and FERPA makes it clear that it requires careful consideration for the data and the context. A "reasonable determination" must be made that a student's identity is "not personally identifiable, whether through single or multiple releases, and taking into account other reasonably available information." ED notes that "deidentification" is considered successful when there is no reasonable basis to believe that the remaining information in the records can be used to identify an individual.[2]

If that sounds like a broad and wide standard, it is. It requires removal of not just the obvious, direct identifiers, such as names and phone numbers, but also consideration for which of the indirect identifiers might need to be removed, such as grade or class schedule, when the sample size or context might cause that information to render an individual identifiable. It also requires attention to what the information will be used for and what other information about an individual is readily available. If a data point is not identifiable when sitting on its own, but could be identifiable when linked to other information about an individual that is readily available, that data point likely needs to be removed or obfuscated from the data set in order to establish the data set as deidentified.

Consideration must also be taken for whether or not the individual would be identifiable in the local community, where indirect identifiers could more easily lead one to pinpoint an individual than they would if shared in a context in which the individual was wholly unknown.

Technology-enabled data collection, if it includes certain biometric data, keystroke data, or other personalized signature elements, also needs to be taken into consideration.

Finally, the risk of reidentification must be considered. If the deidentified data set is disclosed, is there other information that is easily available that could be combined with the deidentified data set to render it identifiable? Can the data set be easily reverted to its original state? If so, then the deidentification work is not complete.

Deidentifying data requires development of protocols that take into account the legal requirements, possible combinations of data elements, size of the data set, other readily available information, and the context in which the deidentified data will be used. There are a variety of technical methods to assist in deidentifying data; however, each school system needs to establish its own protocols given its particular data set, interests in developing and using deidentified data, and existing technical standards.

Record-Keeping Requirements

Any good compliance program has a record-keeping component, and some of that is already built into FERPA requirements. The regulation requires that school systems keep a record of each request for access to and disclosure of personally identifiable information from the education record of each student. Records must also be kept on state and local educational authorities, and on federal agencies and officials that are permitted to disclose personally identifiable information from education records without obtaining prior parent or eligible student consent.

The records must note which parties have requested or received the personally identifiable information from the education records and for what legitimate purpose. These records must be kept for as long as the school system maintains the student's education record, a period of time that is often dictated by the state student data retention laws.

Enforcement

FERPA is enforced by the Family Policy Compliance Office (FPCO) of ED. FPCO is authorized to review complaints it receives alleging noncompliance with FERPA and investigate those complaints as it sees fit. When FPCO finds a school system to be operating in violation of FERPA, it will generally issue notice explaining the specific steps that are necessary and expected in order to comply with the law. It will also establish a time frame within which those steps must be completed.

FERPA is a "spending clause." It is part of the General Education Provisions Act,[3] which requires that school systems meet certain obligations when they receive federal education funds. As such, in the event that a school system does not comply with an enforcement notice, ED has other tools at its disposal to compel compliance. Those include issuing a cease-and-desist order, withholding funding previously provided by ED until compliance is achieved, or terminating a school system's eligibility to receive such funding.

Should ED's investigation reveal that a third party that had received access to personally identifiable student information from education records redisclosed any of that personally identifiable information without obtaining the necessary prior parent or eligible student consents, ED has the authority to require that school system not allow that third party access to personally identifiable information from its education records for at least five years.

PROTECTION OF PUPIL RIGHTS AMENDMENT (PPRA)[4]

The Protection of Pupil Rights Amendment (PPRA) is one of the least-discussed student data privacy laws. Despite its relative obscurity, it provides important guidance and requirements related to collection of sensitive information in the classroom, as well as limitations on use of data for marketing purposes.

PPRA applies to state educational agencies, local educational agencies, or others who receive funding from ED. Like FERPA, PPRA is a spending clause, enforced by the FPCO. Its penalties are quite similar to those in FERPA: investigation and notice of required remedies are enforced in large part by the ability of ED to withhold federal funding or terminate a school system's eligibility to receive federal funding to compel compliance.

Unlike FERPA, which applies rather broadly to the student education record and is particularly concerned with disclosure of personally identifiable information from the education record, PPRA is focused on information collected directly from a student via surveys, analysis, or evaluation of sensitive topics such as

- political affiliations or beliefs of the student or the student's parents;
- mental or psychological problems of the student or the student's family;
- behaviors or attitudes in relation to sexuality;
- illegal, antisocial, self-incriminating, or demeaning behavior;
- critical appraisals of individuals in close familial relationship to the student;
- legally recognized privileged or analogous relationships, such as those of a legal, medical, or political nature;

- religious practices, affiliations, or beliefs of the student or the student's parents; and
- income (other than what is legally permissible to determine eligibility for participation in a program or for receiving financial assistance).

PPRA requires that, in the event that there will be a survey, analysis, evaluation, or similar measure asking students about these sensitive topics, the school system must provide advance notice to parents and obtain their prior consent when that survey is funded in whole or in part by ED. In this sense, while FERPA requires that school system provide parents and eligible students with access to the student's education record, PPRA requires that school systems ask for permission before collecting certain information in the first place.

When a survey involving one of the sensitive topics is not funded by ED, the school system must, at a minimum, provide annual notice to parents at the beginning of the school year about its intent to conduct surveys. That notice must explain the anticipated dates of any such surveys, and allow parents to opt their child out of participation. Parents must also be informed about their right to review instructional materials used in connection with such a survey and as part of the curriculum.

Similar notice must be provided to parents, in advance, of any non-emergency, invasive physical exam or screening when it is required as a condition of attendance, administered by the school, and not necessary to protect the immediate health and safety of any student.

PPRA is also concerned with policy development governing this work. In the event that a school system has not yet established policies for managing the notice and consent process, as well as the process for granting access to the surveys and related instructional materials to parents who request to review the information, the school system must work with parents in the community to develop policies that encompass

- the right of parents to inspect a survey created by the school system or a third party before the survey is administered or distributed to students, and the process for responding to such requests from parents;
- how the school system will protect the privacy of students when the survey contains any of the sensitive topics described above;

- the right of parents to inspect instructional material that is part of the educational curriculum, and how the school system will grant such requests for access;
- administration of physical exams or screenings of students;
- collection, use, and disclosure of personal information when collected from the student for marketing purposes, or to sell or otherwise provide the information to others for marketing purposes, and how the school system will protect student data privacy in the event of such actions; and
- the right of parents to inspect any instrument used in collection from students of personal information for marketing or sales person before the instrument is implemented, and how the school system will provide such access.

The last two bullets related to use of student personal information for marketing purposes are particularly noteworthy. One of the fears regarding student data privacy has been steeped in the question of whether or not FERPA is sufficient to protect student data privacy when the data is collected and managed by technology providers. A specific question has been whether or not technology providers could use personally identifiable student data for marketing purposes.

Looking at the laws, one could argue that it is actually PPRA that holds the key to solving that issue, at least when dealing with information collected from the student. It specifically requires that school systems develop policies related to how they might sell student personal information, how they might collect and use student personal information for marketing purposes, and how they will protect student privacy in such an event.

PPRA does permit use of student personal information for marketing purposes when that marketing is primarily for educational materials and postsecondary pathways. PPRA also allows a school system to collect, use, or disclose student personal information without adhering to the policy-writing requirements of the law when the information is used to develop, evaluate, or provide educational products or services, such as

- college or other postsecondary education or military recruitment;
- cook clubs, magazines, and programs providing access to low-cost literary products;

- curriculum and instructional materials used by elementary and secondary schools;
- tests and assessments used by elementary and secondary schools to provide cognitive, evaluative, diagnostic, clinical, aptitude, or achievement information about students, as well as analysis and release of aggregated results;
- fundraising for school or education-related activities in the form of student sale of products or services; and
- student recognition programs.

However, the mere fact that a law permits certain activities doesn't mean that a school system must engage in those activities. Each school system must determine what they want to deem acceptable. This determination involves a good deal of assessment of not only the laws, but the values, norms, and expectations of the community in which the school system operates, the data-protection capabilities of the school system, the repercussions of restricting or permitting certain legally permissible activities, and a variety of other factors that will be discussed in chapter 6.

In addition, note that none of the laws works in a vacuum. They each need to be considered alongside each other, with attention to where they are complementary and where they conflict. For example, while PPRA has some restrictions and some permissions related to use of student personal information for marketing purposes, it does not preempt state laws, many of which specifically prohibit some marketing activity.

STATE STUDENT DATA PRIVACY LAWS

In the K–12 ecosystem, it's difficult to overstate the impact that state student data privacy laws have had on the landscape. Beginning in 2014, as a result of the existing, unprecedented attention to privacy protections for student data and how school systems were managing their responsibilities and relationships with technology providers, states began writing new student data privacy law. Almost every state has since proposed or passed its own law, and sometimes multiple laws, directly regulating student data privacy.[5] Most of these laws are enforced against technology providers and not school systems, although there are some exceptions.[6]

Since the laws are specific to each state, and since several states have multiple laws covering student data privacy, it would be impossible to catalog all of them here. However, it's imperative that school systems become familiar with their state laws in order to be able to implement the requirements and develop appropriate policies and procedures as part of their data privacy compliance programs.

Unfortunately, many of the laws employ imprecise language and constructs that leave them open to questions on interpretation. Despite that, few states have issued guidance on how the laws should be read and implemented. Those that have issued guidance have not addressed the vagaries of the laws. Consider consulting with your state legislators, state board of education, or state attorney general for specific information and insight into how they are interpreting the laws, and if they will issue official statements to that effect. Also keep in mind that, unlike FERPA and PPRA, state student data privacy laws are applicable broadly and not limited to school systems that receive government funding.

Despite the variety of laws across the states, there are a few common threads applicable to data privacy protections that can be extrapolated. Speaking broadly, the laws tend to focus on protecting the privacy, security, and integrity of student personal information in alignment with the following key concepts:

- control
- access
- restriction
- transparency

Control

Many state student data privacy laws reiterate the existing FERPA requirement that a school system maintain "direct control" over its student personal information when working with technology providers. That control extends to ensuring that when student personal information is collected by or shared with a technology provider, it is used only to serve the school purpose.

In addition, some of the laws specifically ensure that the school system's control, and the limitations in place regarding what the data may be used for, extend to third-party organizations that may partner with technology providers. It is quite common for technology providers to rely on external partners to provide services and support certain product functions. Examples include cloud storage services, data analytics providers, video players, and customer service. In many cases, states laws require that the data privacy and security practices of the technology provider, and the limitations imposed by their agreement with the school system, extend to any of their service providers that may have a need to receive student personal information in order for the technology to operate as expected.

Certain states, notably California, Colorado, Connecticut, Louisiana, and New York, require specific contractual provisions or minimum thresholds for subject matter that must be addressed in agreements between school systems and technology providers.

There are also a variety of provisions in state laws that require technology providers to delete student personal information in their possession when their contract with a school system terminates or within a reasonable time frame after such termination.

Many states also allow students to retain their user-generated content in a personal account, including one that they establish with the technology provider, if the technology provider offers such features.

Access

Access requirements under state laws tend to fall, as expected, on the side of restriction. That is, ensuring that those who receive access to student personal information are only those individuals and entities that need to have it in order to perform a school function. This is, again, aligned with the requirements of FERPA that school systems define what they consider to be a legitimate educational interest that may qualify an entity as a school official and provide school officials with only the personally identifiable student information in which they have a legitimate educational interest. It is also aligned with long-standing, fundamental privacy concepts.

Some state laws have been designed to speak to specific, modern-day access scenarios, such as to ensure that school systems do not compel students to provide their passwords for personal devices or social media accounts.

Many laws also reiterate existing parent access rights under FERPA, ensuring that parents maintain their rights to access, review, and request to amend or correct errors in their child's education record.

Restrictions

A critical difference between the federal and state student data privacy laws is the state focus on restricting data use for commercial purposes. It is very common to see state laws that prohibit use of student personal information for the purpose of engaging in "targeted advertising" to students, and in some cases, to parents and teachers as well.

"Targeted advertising" is terminology that first appeared—but was not defined—in California's Student Online Personal Information Protection Act (SOPIPA). Under SOPIPA, technology providers covered by the law are prohibited from engaging in targeted advertising "when the targeting of the advertising is based upon any information, including covered information and persistent unique identifiers, that the operator has acquired because of the use of that operator's site, service or application."[7] Since that time, a variety of states have copied this language. In some cases, the language has been refined to get closer to a clearer definition of what activities are and are not restricted.

What is clear is that states are concerned with the potential for data to be used for marketing purposes. Concerns about marketing to young people is as old as the dawn of Saturday-morning cartoons. Young children are vulnerable populations, afforded special regulatory protections, and there is longstanding regulation in the media sector intended to address the issue. However, in the education sector, the restrictions have moved beyond past concerns that were focused on marketing to children. In the case of states such as California, marketing to adults has also been restricted when student data is used for such marketing.

Regardless of where the definitions and interpretations of these provisions end up, it is clear that many state laws conflict with certain permissive provisions in PPRA.

State laws also tend to prohibit the sale of student personal information, with exceptions made in the event that a technology provider is sold or undergoes another comparable change in ownership. In those cases, the laws account for the fact that the data may move with the sale.

However, while the laws often permit the data to move to the new owner-ship entity, they often stipulate, as is commonly required across some existing legal frameworks, that it must remain subject to the previously existing data protection agreements.

Transparency

Overarching all of the requirements is an interest in renewed or additional transparency about how student personal information is protected. A variety of laws require state education agencies and school systems to develop data governance policies to help further protect the privacy of student data and, in some cases, to develop uniform requirements for such protections across the state. Such policies are usually expected to be publicly available, easily accessible to parents.

In many cases, state educational agencies must document what data they collect from and about students, and school systems must make clear what technology providers they are working with. In certain states, the laws require that contracts with technology providers be made publicly available.

Still others take a different approach. New York state law incorporates a requirement that school systems implement a "parents' bill of rights" explain-ing what data is collected and shared, how it is protected, and the limitations on its use. That bill of rights must be made publicly available on the school system website and incorporated into contracts with technology providers.[8]

Some of the laws reiterate already-existing legal requirements to ensure that material changes to privacy policies are not implemented without a tech-nology provider first delivering notice and obtaining prior consent.

Another key area of transparency involves notification in the event of unauthorized access to student personal information that constitutes a security breach. Some states have implemented requirements that, in addition to exist-ing notification requirements to impacted individuals, school systems must also notify state authorities of data breaches within a defined time period.

Enforcement

Penalties for violating state student data privacy laws vary widely. Although already in effect, some of the laws are actually unfinished and include clauses requiring exploration and development of additional material to address unanswered questions, including enforcement.

Many of the laws are enforced against technology providers, with penalties being drawn from each state's existing business codes. Those penalties often include monetary fines and, in extreme cases, could result in revocation of a business license.

However, school systems are not entirely in the clear. Some of the laws have been incorporated into state education codes, and regardless, it's critically important to consult your own state laws on this matter and understand the specific requirements for your school system.

There is wide variation in other clauses across the states, as well as in penalties, with some being quite severe. (In Louisiana, noncompliance may result in monetary fines and prison.[9])

CHILDREN'S ONLINE PRIVACY PROTECTION ACT (COPPA)[10]

COPPA does not apply to, and is not enforced against, school systems. It does apply to technology providers operating commercial websites and online services directed in whole or in part to children, defined as individuals under age thirteen, that collect, use, or disclose personal information from children. It also applies to operators of general audience sites and services with actual knowledge that they are collecting, using, or disclosing personal information from children, and to operators of sites and online services that have actual knowledge that they are collecting personal information directly from users of another site or service directed to children.

COPPA was written with specific concern about data collection from children for marketing purposes in mind, and that is reflected in the requirements. It is enforced by the Federal Trade Commission (FTC) and state attorneys general against technology providers.

COPPA requires that technology providers obtain verifiable parental consent before collecting personal information from a child under the age of thirteen. When a contract exists between a school system and a technology provider, and when the personal information is to be collected only for the use and benefit of the school and for no other commercial purpose, the technology provider may presume that the school's authorization for the collection of the students' personal information, by virtue of signing the contract, is based on the school having obtained parental consent. However, the operator is required to provide the school system with notice about its data collection, use, and disclosure practices in advance of any such agreement.[11]

If the operator would like to use the student's personal information for other commercial purposes, the operator is required to make the request for that permission directly to the parent or legal guardian. When such commercial use is restricted by state student data privacy laws, the state prohibition would hold.

In addition, COPPA requires that operators collect only the minimally required personal information necessary to provide a service or feature, not condition a child's participation in an activity on providing information not necessary to fulfill that activity, provide reasonable security, and ensure that its third-party operators do the same.

Under COPPA, operators must also allow parents to review the types or categories of personal information collected from their child. Parents must also be given the opportunity to review the personal information collected from their child, and may refuse to allow the operator to make further use of their child's personal information or to delete it. However, in such an event, the operator may, when necessary, then revoke the provision of the services to the child if they cannot be provided without the child's personal information.

Parent rights under COPPA are important for school systems to understand, as parents requesting an operator delete the child's personal information may interfere with the education record when the technology is used in the classroom. A good practice, then, is that the school system establish a process to coordinate with the operator and parents to ensure that parent rights are honored but that the school system maintains a copy of all necessary elements of the education record.

COPPA is enforced against operators with statutory penalties of up to $40,654 per violation.[12] In addition, it is not uncommon for the FTC to require that violators delete the data they collected in violation of the law, to implement annual privacy training, and to submit to annual third-party compliance audits, often under multi-year consent decrees. All of the laws use different terms and definitions for the information that is to be protected.

Legal Definitions of Protected Information

When considering how to define the scope of student personal information that needs to be protected in your school system, it's important to note that different laws define personal information in different ways, and using different nomenclature. Here are a few important examples:

Family Educational Rights and Privacy Act

Personally Identifiable Information: Includes, but is not limited to the student's

- name;
- name(s) of parent(s) or other family members;
- address or family's address;
- personal identifiers, such as Social Security number, student number, or biometric record;
- indirect identifiers, such as date of birth, place of birth, and mother's maiden name;
- information that, alone or in combination, is linked or linkable to him or her that would allow a reasonable person in the school community, who does not have personal knowledge of the relevant circumstances, to identify him or her with reasonable certainty; and
- information requested by a person who the educational institution reasonably believes to know the identity of the student to whom the education record relates.

Children's Online Privacy Protection Act.

Personal Information: Individually identifiable information collected online from a child under the age of thirteen, including

- first and last name;
- address or other geolocation information that identifies a street name and city or town;
- email address or other online contact information such as a screen or user name that allows direct online contact with the child;
- telephone number;
- Social Security number;
- persistent identifiers that can be used to recognize the child over time and across different websites or online services[a];
- photographs, videos, or audio files that contain the child's image or voice; and

- information about the child or the child's parents or legal guardians that the operator collects online from the child and combines with one or more of the above identifiers.

State Laws

Many state laws intend to protect what they refer to as "covered information," which is usually defined as "personally identifiable information." However, what constitutes "personally identifiable information" under state student-data privacy laws is commonly left undefined.

What is clear is that state student-data privacy laws intend to protect student personally identifiable information shared with the technology provider by the student, parent, school system, or office of education, regardless of what media or format it appears in. State laws also commonly intend to protect information that is collected directly by the technology provider through the operation of their product or service that is "descriptive or a student or otherwise identifies a student."[b]

[a]"Children's Online Privacy Protection Act," https://www.ecfr.gov/cgi-bin/text-idx?SID=4939e77c77a1a1a0 8c1cbf905fc4b409&node=16%3A1.0.1.3.36&rgn=div5. Although the persistent identifier that can be used to recognize a user over time and across different websites or online services is personal information under COPPA, operators subject to COPPA are not required to obtain prior consent to collect the persistent identifier and use it for specific functions deemed support for the internal operations. These are activities necessary to:

(a) maintain or analyze the functioning of the website or online service;
(b) perform network communications;
(c) authenticate users of, or personalize the content on, the website or online service;
(d) serve contextual advertising on the website or online service or cap the frequency of advertising;
(e) protect the security or integrity of the user, website, or online service;
(f) ensure legal or regulatory compliance; or
(g) fulfill a request of a child as permitted by §§ 312.5(c)(3) and (4);
so long as the information collected for the activities listed in paragraphs (a)–(g) is not used or disclosed to contact a specific individual, including through behavioral advertising, to amass a profile on a specific individual, or for any other purpose.

[b]"Student Online Personal Information Protection Act," https://leginfo.legislature.ca.gov/faces/billNavClient. xhtml?bill_id=201320140SB1177.

STILL MORE LAWS

There are other laws that are not primarily concerned with student data privacy, but that include considerations for it.

The Children's Internet Protection Act (CIPA)[13] is not specifically a data protection law, however implementing CIPA does bring about certain data-privacy questions that need to be addressed.

CIPA is enforced by the Federal Communications Commission. It applies to schools and libraries that receive discounts for Internet access or internal connections through the E-rate program. In order to qualify for the E-rate discounts, school systems and libraries must implement an Internet safety policy that includes technology protections that block or filter Internet access to child pornography and pictures that are obscene or harmful to minors where the computer is accessed by minors. That policy must also address, the safety and security of minors when using direct electronic communications, such as email and chat rooms, hacking and other forms of unauthorized online access and unlawful activities by minors online, unauthorized disclosure, use and dissemination of personal information regarding minors, and measures restricting access by minors of materials deemed harmful to them.

School systems must also ensure that they educate their minor students about appropriate online behavior, including interacting on social media and in chat rooms and cyberbullying awareness and response. Internet safety policies must include monitoring of minor students' online activities.

Monitoring online activities requires data collection and, with that, consideration for the previously noted laws. Development of a CIPA compliance plan needs to be aligned with a general data privacy compliance program in order to create appropriate rules and contractual protections with a technology provider delivering the monitoring services about how the data collected through the monitoring program will be managed, who will have access, and how long it will be stored.

The National Student Lunch Act[14] makes clear that only individuals who need to know information about applications to the program in order to properly implement, record, or audit the program receive it. The privacy of those students eligible for free and reduced meal service is paramount.

In addition, it is possible that some school system student data may be subject to the Health Insurance Portability and Accountability Act (HIPAA). HIPAA may apply if the school system is processing certain electronic transactions, applying to health plans, or any number of other transactional situations involving health data. However, for elementary and secondary schools, the student health information maintained by the school system is commonly subject to FERPA.[15] There are exceptions, however, so as always, it's important to consult with the laws and available guidance.

BEYOND THE LAWS

Properly managing compliance with the laws is not the only reason why a student data privacy compliance program is a necessary component of the modern school system. A data privacy compliance program sets expectations for behavior, showcases leadership understanding of the importance of protecting student data privacy, creates frameworks to ensure student data privacy remains protected even as new technologies come into the classroom, and builds efficiency for addressing student data privacy concerns while continuing to modernize the school system.

A mature data privacy compliance program also ensures more consistency between the school system mission, vision, and its use of data; decreases human errors that compromise data security; and builds awareness across the school system, mobilizing all employees to properly protect the privacy of student data.

If that is not sufficiently motivating, also consider, for example, the financial repercussions of not having a proper compliance program in place.

It is sometimes tempting to rely on the fact that the enforcement penalties of FERPA and PPRA, whereby ED may withhold federal funding or terminate a school system's eligibility to receive federal funding, have never been implemented. It can create a false sense of security, or perhaps simply make it more difficult to make a strong case in your school system for developing a proper student data privacy compliance program.

The risk in that, however, is that should ED receive a complaint regarding your school system's compliance with the laws, they may start an investigation. Whether you are found to be operating in compliance or not, the investigation alone can be an unwieldy proposition.

Responding to any regulatory action is expensive. It triggers an incalculable amount of man hours gathering information, documenting practices, and more, usually with support and oversight of legal counsel. While that is going on, the routine work is sitting unattended.

Regulatory investigations are not often conducted swiftly. Government agencies are not resourced with armies of investigators that can hustle you through the process, and there is bureaucracy to lumber through before final findings can be issued. What if you are the subject of an investigation that lingers? Are you prepared for the disruption?

In addition, if a school system is found to be out of compliance with the laws, impact on a bond application or other state or local funding opportunities can be disastrous, even without enforcement penalties. While this is all happening, parents in the district will be at the doorstep, demanding answers. Yet more time, energy, and effort will be needed to respond, requiring resources you may not have available.

It is followed by the potential that ED will issue findings and requirements to bring the school system into compliance. More hours will need to be spent building a compliance program in accordance with the government's imposed schedule, not yours. It can cause tremendous upheaval in any organization, and it can be quite costly.

If a technology provider causes you to fall out of compliance, you are precluded from providing them with student data for five years. For the technology provider, the repercussions and reverberations in the marketplace will have just begun. The school system will be left with the task of searching for a replacement product. If the technology provider was a student information system or other critical operational technology, how would you be poised to move swiftly to identify a qualified replacement, make a smooth transition to the new provider, and be up and running without downtime or other impact on your operations?

While you can't always prevent an investigation from starting, the best-case scenario is that in the event that the regulators do come calling, your policies, processes, and practices are documented, auditable, and available at your fingertips. In addition, you'll ideally have built trust within your community such that parents understand how you protect the privacy of student data.

With confidence in your existing practices, readily available documentation, fluency in the regulations and a reasonably trustworthy parent community, you will be better positioned to have productive discussions with the regulators, and be able to bring about a swifter resolution with less disruption, while maintaining some community trust.

Security Incidents

One needs to look no further than the daily news to know that data security incidents in the form of unauthorized access to sensitive, personal information are now a regular occurrence. The truth is that there is no such thing as a completely secure data system, impervious to intruders. However, what can be accomplished is a reasonable framework, designed with attention to current industry best practices and encompassing technological, physical, and administrative safeguards.

Note that the technology alone will not provide reasonable security standards. In fact, human error accounts for more data security incidents than technology errors.[16] Consider the following: an administrative assistant leaves a thumb drive with sensitive data on a desk, a teacher leaves his password next to the laptop for convenience, an administrator accidentally sends a file with sensitive information to the wrong distribution list, an engineer inadvertently introduces errors into code, or a superintendent leaves a laptop in a car that gets broken into. These are very real examples of the human behaviors that have led to data security incidents in school systems.

These incidents can be quite costly. As with regulatory investigations, the hard costs are accompanied by variable and opportunity costs. Consider that managing a data security incident often involves legal fees, cost of engagement with an external forensics firm, costs of notifying state regulators and impacted individuals, and often providing credit-monitoring services. In addition, there are the man-hour costs of investigating, containing, and mitigating an incident, plus crafting communications for parents and press. In the aftermath of an incident, insurance premiums may rise, and enrollment may decline, taking with it a loss of funding. All the while, parents may very well be losing their trust in your ability to protect their children.

A compliance program that includes rules of behavior, training, policies, and processes will not prevent all security incidents, but it can reduce the likelihood and frequency of certain types of events occurring. It can also increase the efficiency and comprehensiveness with which incidents are addressed. It is often said that it is only a matter of time before every organization experiences a data security incident. Without a compliance program, security incidents may be all but guaranteed. With one, the frequency and severity of any incident may be greatly decreased, and with it, the costs.[17]

Reputational Harm

Once the dust settles and the bills are paid, the damage lingers in the form of reputational harm. Results of investigations by FPCO are often posted publicly.[18] Press reports about security incidents often spread before a school system even has a real handle on the scope of the situation. The FTC makes all of its settlements related to noncompliance with COPPA public,[19] and state attorneys general do as well, both via press releases and other public postings, which are often widely reported in the media.

If the compliance issue stemmed from a school system, or if a technology provider's product or service used by the school system is implicated in a regulatory action, the school system's reputation may be in jeopardy.

While the school system is responding to a regulatory inquiry, working with counsel, reallocating teams to address the compliance requirements, reallocating budgets to attempt to cover the costs, working with an insurance provider to defray some costs, or possibly finding a new vendor to provide critical services, the community may be demanding answers. If we've learned anything from past concerns related to student data privacy in schools, it's that delayed responses can exacerbate the problem. Time is of the essence.

It's Your Responsibility

Parents trust that you will care for the safety of their children, and with the modern classroom, *that fundamental responsibility for care extends to protecting student data.* In fact, this entire section about "why build a compliance program" could be stated most simply as: "when we choose to work with students or handle data from or about students, we have an inherent responsibility to protect their information."

It's no secret that parents have questions about how technology is used in school systems. In the modern age, our data is an extension of who we are, and parents want assurances that their child's identifiable data will be used only to support their child.

Question topics that might be top-of-mind for parents in your community may include

- the validity and efficacy of using technology as a teaching tool;
- the risk of their children accessing inappropriate content;
- whether or not the use of technology in schools results in too much screen time;
- what happens with information gathered from and about their children via the use of technology;
- how the school system controls the use of data shared with technology providers; and
- why a particular data incident occurred, who was impacted, what are the risks of harm, and what is being done to prevent it in the future.

There are no easy answers to these questions, and certainly no "one size fits all" solution. However, there are facts that can be provided, in plain language that are easy for parents to understand. Those facts can go a long way toward reassuring parents that the school system is informed, capable, and competent to manage a technology-enabled classroom. In order to be able to provide that information, one must be fluent in the requirements and ensure that the information is backed up by comparable action. Words are not enough. There must be a tangible, demonstrable program of action.

Trust is earned. Brick by brick and moment by moment. Even in the absence of data security incidents and regulatory action, data privacy is a complex topic and parents are often overwhelmed by the sheer volume and pervasiveness of technology in their children's lives, as well as by the look and feel of the modern classroom. If you have not established a robust and comprehensive data privacy compliance program and made a concerted effort to inform your community about the work you've done and the attention you've paid, in a way that they can easily understand, you've not built trust.

As a result, time and energy will be expended providing reassurances to worried parents, instead of collaborating together to build a better education for students. Moving ahead with innovative technologies will be challenged. In addition, if and when you have a data incident, you will have no foundation of trust to ease the conversation with your community members, who will be hard-pressed to believe that an incident was an aberration, and not a symptom of a larger problem.

A compliance program is a risk-mitigation strategy. It can reduce not just the risk of an adverse event occurring but also the costs of an adverse event should one arise. It is also a component of what it takes to live up to the fundamental responsibility of providing a proper standard of care to students.

Chapter 4

What Does It Take?

Building a data privacy compliance program is not a small endeavor. It often requires establishing a new function for the organization, with leadership and, within the constraints of available resources, appropriately qualified staff to develop, implement, and oversee the work. The function, by its nature, has a reach and exposure that threads through almost every team in the school system that has access to or makes use of data. When implemented properly, it is constructive, mission-driven, and solutions-oriented and comprehensive.

A compliance program is meant to work in partnership with other teams, supporting positive and effective uses of data while building policies and processes that enable the teams to steer away from risk. Those policies and processes need to be realistic given the size and scope of the organization and the sensitivity of the data. They also need to be easy to implement, not unduly disruptive to existing and often well-entrenched workflows.

The compliance function is a center point of knowledge and information about privacy, responsible for ensuring that leadership and staff are educated on roles, responsibilities, laws, and the greater landscape in which the school system operates.

The first step to getting there is to consider how such a function will be established. Are there individuals on staff who have privacy expertise? Do you need to bring in leadership or find qualified outside resources to help train existing staff to take on new responsibilities? Consider what education, training, and depth of experience is needed to establish and implement a data privacy compliance program in your school system.

Establish goals for the compliance program. What is it that you want to accomplish? You may want to create an overarching mission and vision for the program, as well as annual and incremental, project-based goals.

With the goals in mind, a scope of work can be developed. It may begin with understanding current practices and what employees do and don't know about the requirements, how well existing policies and processes are implemented, and how success of those policies is measured. It will also encompass what data collection and storage tools and technologies are built and maintained by the school system, from websites to networks to servers. Ultimately, the work will move to improving or creating a comprehensive set of policies and practices that govern the collection, handling, storage, use, disclosure, and deletion of data across the school system.

Building a compliance program also involves assessing the compliance practices of those with whom you share student personal information, including technology providers. The controls you have in place over student personal information when it's shared with third parties and how you bring technology into your building also need to be reviewed or established.

All of this must be evaluated, first to establish the benchmarks: to assess where things currently sit in relation to the laws, community expectations, and district policies. Gaps must be identified between existing policies and processes and stated goals. Those gaps must in turn be reviewed to understand what of the risks are most critical, with the most severe repercussions and the strongest probability of occurrence.

Gaps should then be ranked in accordance with risk, likelihood that those risks will come to fruition, and available resources to address them. Remediation plans for gaps need to be established, with strategies for implementing the plans and then, of course, the implementation needs to commence.

Remediation plans need to be created to address existing issues and to create new policies and procedures so that the same issues aren't created in the future. Training is then required on new policies and procedures so that all employees understand their roles and responsibilities in managing compliance.

As with any work, it's important to establish metrics for success. Consider how you will quantify the efficacy of the compliance work. On an annual basis, quantify and capture those metrics, then review those measurements against the goals and adjust the program accordingly.

Transparency is also a key component of a compliance program. Educating parents, students, and other community members about the program, the ways in which you protect the privacy of student data, and the role they have to play as responsible users of technology is an often overlooked but important component. They are stakeholders in a school system compliance program. Their support is critical, but it will only be earned by being transparent about what you are doing, what you hope to achieve, and how they can contribute.

Compliance is never perfect and never finished. It is a process of ongoing assessment and improvement. Laws change, the climate shifts, technologies evolve, and the policies and practices put into place need to be evaluated regularly to determine effectiveness. Modifications, even small adjustments, may be needed to build on any existing foundation of compliance and improve upon it.

It is a lot to cover, and none of it can be put into place or maintained effectively without leadership engagement.

Chapter 5

The Role of Leadership

A successful compliance program depends on support from leadership. It must be championed and prioritized across the organization from the top. Leadership sets the tone and expectations, empowering employees involved in the daily operations to implement policies and procedures properly.

While many in a school system may identify the need to build a data privacy compliance program, leadership must launch the effort and convey the importance and the "why" behind it.

BUILD MEANING

When done well, compliance sits in alignment with a school system's mission and vision. Unfortunately, compliance is often implemented as an exercise of looking at the legal requirements, figuring out the policies and processes to help the school system align with those requirements, and requiring that all employees follow those rules. Check the boxes and be done.

However, that type of compliance often fails. It doesn't take into consideration the complexity of the requirements and the potential disruption new policies and processes often cause. It is a narrow view of requirements, handed down as obligation for the teams, often without context. It rarely captures the nuances of daily operations or situational issues and exceptions that arise or includes guidance on how to handle them. It also doesn't incorporate the rigorous auditing and accountability measures required in order to assess whether or not the work is effective.

"Check the box compliance" also ignores community norms, expectations, and active decision-making around what is appropriate in the local setting and doesn't adequately motivate employees to consistently follow the policies and processes.

The truth is that a compliance program can be inspired or tired. When it's tired, boring, or inconvenient, efforts to comply don't last long. Inconvenience trumps implementation, and employees quickly look for ways to avoid following procedure. This is particularly common when there is no mission-driven rationale behind the program.

Protecting the privacy of student data requires ongoing monitoring, vigilance, review, and adjustment. It is a living, breathing function. Much of the life of the program comes from the employees who implement the policies and processes on a daily basis. Turn the test papers facedown so that students can't see each other's grades, use the secure system to send sensitive information, close the laptop before leaving the room. These habits develop over time, and getting to a place where these actions are routine takes planning and training.

If motivation for doing the work is created through the stick of "it's the law" instead of the carrot of "it's part of who we are as responsible educators," it conveys that leadership is doing it "because we have to," not because it's the right thing to do and we believe in it."

When the rationale for building a compliance program is inspired by a larger mission behind the action, it takes on meaning and significance. The law is an important part of it, but not the only part. With leadership articulating a mission-driven rationale as the framework, teams are better able to connect the requirements to their roles and responsibilities, taking on ownership of their part in protecting student data privacy.

AUTHORIZE AND EMPOWER

Leadership needs to recognize the resources required to build an effective compliance program and ensure that they are provided at appropriate levels. Compliance can be a cost center. It requires an investment of time, dollars, and attention. However, a good compliance program does bring cost savings in the event of regulatory action, an incident, or addressing parent concerns. When done well, a good compliance program is designed to put a school system out ahead of the issues. It ensures that risks are identified, contained, and addressed. This results in real cost savings to any institution when one considers the often extraordinary man hours that can be involved when managing a crisis.

Compliance also builds efficiency in operations. When implemented properly, a good compliance team identifies boundaries of what is permitted and what is restricted. With proper training and controls, these guideposts often allow employees broad range within which to operate cleanly.

Compliance is also not a single-stakeholder endeavor. Almost every individual in a school system touches student data in some way and so has a role to play in safeguarding that data. It might be a teacher in the classroom handling attendance and test scores; an athletic coach observing behavior, fitness, and health issues; an administrative assistant processing transcripts; or a guidance counselor addressing social issues.

While an individual needs to be in charge of data privacy compliance, the responsibilities and requirements will flow across multiple teams. Leadership needs to set the tone and deliver the expectation that all teams will participate and cooperate and explain how that will happen.

Without the voice of leadership, an individual employee or team has the challenge of trying to develop and oversee policies and processes for all teams that touch student data or that bring in technology that will touch student data. Imagine having no agency or authority over other teams in a school system, but being required to develop rules of behavior for all of them. It would require countless hours of courtship, establishing the importance of the work with each team, gaining buy-in and approval from each team to proceed, balancing different team priorities and schedules, and navigating politics and personalities.

While all of that is still part of the process, without leadership spearheading the initiative, it's doomed to fail. At best, it utilizes precious time and resources across all teams simply to get to a place where there is agreement to participate.

Instead, leadership must champion the work. By recognizing the importance of protecting the privacy of student data and accepting that accomplishing that aim requires a commitment to embark on a complex process to uncover issues and create a new pathway forward for the future, leadership can best communicate the need for the initiative across the entire school system. Leadership can also quickly establish for the entire ecosystem that everyone is expected to engage in the work under the direction of a designated individual or team.

Regardless of how it's structured, and whether it is a team of one or many, it's important to appreciate that data privacy compliance is its own complex and rather large function. It reaches across the organization to develop, launch, enforce, measure, and educate on policies and processes that touch all employees. It needs to complement existing functions and not burden an already taxed team with new and unfamiliar responsibilities. It requires advance planning and thoughtfulness surrounding how building a privacy compliance program might impact existing budgets, workloads, and operations.

BE ACCOUNTABLE

Leadership is ultimately responsible for what happens in a school system. Whether it's improving graduation rates or protecting student data privacy, leadership can take the credit or will get the blame. In the event of regulatory action, unauthorized access to student personal information, or a parent community upset over a technology program, leadership will be called to answer for it. It's best then, that leadership have clear, informed expectations about how they want the school system to approach such a critical effort.

MAKING THE CASE TO LEADERSHIP

It's easy to say that leadership should prioritize and champion data privacy compliance efforts. The reality, of course, is that this isn't always how things start. Leadership may be balancing other critical priorities. They may also not be fluent in the specifics of data collection, storage, handling, and disclosure practices, or even with the volume of technology used in individual classrooms.

Certainly there are a variety of very technical specifications and requirements inherent in managing the modern classroom that require individuals with specific expertise to handle them properly. One doesn't expect leadership to be a subject matter expert in all of them.

What leadership must do, however, is recognize and respond to the risk and responsibility when they are made aware of it.

It is certainly likely that school system leadership understands fundamental legal regulations and that protecting student data privacy is important. However, if a data privacy compliance program hasn't been established or if an established program isn't operating well, leadership needs to be made aware.

It is sometimes the chief technology officer, chief security officer, information specialist, or engineering team that will recognize the need to build or overhaul a compliance program. Since that work is not practical and not usually successful without leadership support, a very common question that arises at that point is: How does one make the case to leadership?

A compelling case can be built by understanding how your superintendent and board make decisions, what will be most meaningful to them, making the information you present directly relevant to your school system operations and, with that in mind, developing a proposal for getting the program started.

Know Your Audience

Regardless of the subject matter, making a case to leadership for any project in any industry is, in some ways, a marketing exercise. You have an idea that you'd like leadership to take on and champion. How do you get them engaged enough to want to build a compliance program, or to at least agree to take up the gauntlet? What would be meaningful from their perspective?

Consider the current and overarching leadership priorities. Are budgets tight? If so, how can a compliance program save money in the long term? Is student success a pressing goal? If so, how will protecting their data properly allow you to use the data more effectively, perhaps to identify issues and intervene to better support students, or to open up more opportunities for them? Is your leadership risk averse? If so, what do they know about the risks inherent in the way the school system currently collects, uses, and otherwise manages student personal information? What about the risks in the education ecosystem at large? What are the one or two leadership priorities you can align with to create a compelling case to build a compliance program?

How does your leadership usually make decisions? Do you need to get other stakeholders involved to support the effort and present to leadership as a group? Or is a solo approach more appropriate? Does leadership rely on certain trusted colleagues for advice? If so, can you ask those individuals for guidance about what sort of approach leadership would appreciate, or the best way to present the information you believe leadership needs to be aware of?

Would your leadership be interested in hearing from leaders in other school systems about how they've prioritized protecting student data privacy? Who should you engage with to help you craft the most compelling and targeted presentation?

Begin with the End in Mind

What is it that you ultimately want to ask of your school system leadership? Is it for support to build a compliance program or improve an existing program? Is it for leadership to begin writing policy and establishing the requirements and expectations for a compliance program? Define what you will be asking for and use the presentation to make your case.

Once you've given some thought to the approach and goal, consider what content to present. There's no right way to do this. However, it's helpful to leverage what you know about how your current leadership makes decisions to inform how you will approach shaping your message. One of the most important questions to consider is why hasn't leadership spearheaded development of a data privacy compliance program just yet? The answer to that question is what you likely need to address if you are to convince leadership to engage on the issue.

Make It Relevant and Real

It's easy to put together a presentation outlining all of the legal requirements. The question to ask is, will that move your leadership team into action? Sometimes a more compelling discussion will focus on (1) direct, present risks to the school system and to leadership and (2) what is required of leadership to support the work.

You and your leadership already know the repercussions for not complying with the laws. Take the information discussed above and quantify it with costs that are directly applicable to your school system. For example, if ED had cause to investigate your school system, what sort of legal fees might be incurred? Would you be able to easily gather your data protection and handling policies and processes? Are they already documented? If not, how many man hours might you spend pulling together that information? Do you have a relationship with qualified counsel you could engage with? What would that cost in terms of salaries and time away from other critical work?

Review the ED's Letters of Importance.[1] Are there any that are particularly relevant to situations that your school system has experienced in the past? If so, that may be helpful as well.

Present information about the costs of not complying. A variety of free resources are available that outline the costs of a data breach,[2] the prevalence of data breaches, and common threats.[3] Most of these resources can be indexed to focus only on the education sector. Find reports of incidents in your state or in neighboring states, and search for situations that might have resulted from risks you foresee as being realistic issues in your school system.

Press reports on security incidents are also compelling material. They often make quite clear that leadership will be the public face of communications about a data security breach. Their engagement is unavoidable, so best to ensure that they are keenly aware of existing risks and that any risk-mitigation program must be implemented with their support and guidance.

If it is permissible in your school system, consider conducting an ethical phishing exercise. Baseline results, along with an explanation of ransomware or other advanced attacks that can result from something as simple as an employee opening a link in an email, may be useful in illustrating the concerns to your school system leadership.

Be Solutions-Oriented

Leadership in any organization is used to hearing about problems. Understanding risk and what could go wrong is part of the work of leadership. Deliver a presentation that addresses not just the risks but the opportunities as well. Articulate how building a compliance program will allow you to better protect student data and deliver on the school system's overall mission. Document this with metrics, and then go beyond the numbers to include other benefits.

Convey that building a compliance program is not just about risk mitigation but also about collaborating with leadership to define your purpose with respect to the data that you do collect. Discuss any questions you've received from parents and lay the groundwork for how building a compliance program will help to build a stronger and more constructive relationship with your local community. Also explain how you propose to make that happen.

Finally, note how your school system leadership can support the work. What is it that they need to do? Have some suggested next steps ready to spark discussion and keep the momentum going.

To recap, your presentation to leadership should be sensitive to the way business is conducted in your school system, and may benefit from

- taking into consideration how leadership is most receptive to proposals;
- recognizing that you may have more technical savvy and insight into potential risks than leadership;
- engaging with trusted colleagues to build support for your proposal, when appropriate;
- being clear about what you are asking leadership to do;
- drawing from legal requirements and information about recent security incidents to build a presentation that is tangible and relevant to your school system;
- discussing benefits and opportunities as much as risk;
- including information about how you propose to proceed; and
- being prepared to discuss the next steps.

Regardless of how you make your case to leadership, the important thing is to make it. Leadership may not even be aware that you are struggling to find the way to make a case for what you believe is needed. However, if you are aware of risks, it is your responsibility to raise them to those who will ultimately bear responsibility for accepting or mitigating those risks.

Chapter 6

Start Where You Are

Whether you are building your first compliance program or are interested in improving an existing program, start where you are. You may have already completed some of the exercises explained in this section, or you may feel compelled to get right to the risk assessment in chapter 8, and come back at a later date to define the big-picture goals. If so, you may find it helpful to jump around through different chapters to piece the material together in the order that works best for you.

However you choose to digest the next few chapters, do read through it in order at least once. If you haven't built a data privacy compliance program yet, it'll help you understand how to build it within the context of larger school system goals and establish a firm foundation for the future. If you have already established the basics of a data privacy compliance program, this section will hopefully spark thought and ideas about how to improve your program, and amplify existing efforts.

CREATE THE ROLE

As with all organizational functions, someone needs to be in charge. Ideally, a qualified chief privacy officer or compliance officer is identified to run the program. All too often, however, unqualified or underqualified individuals are slotted into this role without proper training or experience. A common scenario is to simply add "privacy" to the list of job responsibilities for the existing chief technology officer, chief security officer, IT director, or similar role but not provide them with the education, training, and resources needed to be effective. Unfortunately, the description alone does not bring with it the training to get the job done!

Just as with every other role in a school system, the individual designated as the leader of the compliance program must have the experience, knowledge, authority, and bandwidth to perform the job properly. This person needs to be able to make decisions and be attentive to the ongoing work of protecting student data privacy and should be responsible for enforcing, monitoring, and improving the program. Some fundamental qualifications may include

- fluency in the implementation of FERPA, PPRA, COPPA, CIPA, your state student-data privacy requirements, and fundamental security practices;
- fluency in state education code and data reporting requirements;
- experience as a policy writer;
- adeptness at leading teams and working collaboratively across multiple disciplines;
- a detail-oriented disposition and ability to think conceptually;
- excellent communication skills;
- the ability to translate complex regulatory requirements into actionable policies and processes; and
- the ability to apply existing regulation to new and emerging technologies.

Of course, as with every job, it is not always possible to identify an individual with all of the right qualifications and experience. It is also possible, and even probable, that resources are too tight to create a new role. If that's the case, there are other avenues that can prove to be just as effective.

For example, perhaps you may be able to reorganize an existing technology or security team to make room for that team's leader to take on privacy responsibilities. A small budget, far less than a new salary, could then be invested for education and training for that individual. A virtual chief privacy officer can also be brought on board. This is a qualified privacy expert responsible for building your compliance program while training and empowering existing teams to manage it on their own in the near future. There are also a variety of free training resources available that can at least get someone started on the path to working on privacy issues.[1]

WHAT DO YOU WANT TO DO WITH DATA?

Once the role has been created, it's time to settle into the task of building an effective compliance program. "Effective" means that it protects the privacy of student data, becomes a real and robust function within the school system, is measurable and embedded with accountability framework is reviewed or audited regularly and improved as needed, includes relevant training for all employees, and provides not only policies and procedures but also a touchstone or lens through which to make decisions about data.

Building the program is a team effort. You may benefit from pulling together a committee to inform the broad strokes, including leadership, the newly appointed privacy officer, and parent representatives. This isn't a committee to run the program or even to develop the policies, but a group to develop what is essentially the program charter, or the defined reason for being and primary goals.

Whether you are just getting started with building your school system compliance program or are hoping to improve the one you have, success is easier to achieve when there is a reason for people to follow the rules that is bigger than mitigating risk. That reason should also help empower individuals and teams to make smart, consistent decisions about data use that benefit the students they collectively support.

How does one infuse meaning into protecting student data privacy and inspire teams to attend to it day in and day out? Bring it to life with an ethical, mission-driven backbone.

Working with your committee, connect the establishment of a student data privacy compliance program to the school system's larger mission or vision to inform why the school system collects data and how it will use the data in alignment with the inherent responsibility school systems have to support their students.

Schools have some wonderfully inspiring missions and visions. "All youth achieving."[2] "Every student in every neighborhood will be engaged in a rigorous, well-rounded instructional program and will graduate prepared for success in college, career, and life."[3] "Committed to developing productive citizens prepared to compete in a global community."[4] "All students progress in school and graduate prepared to succeed and contribute in a global diverse society."[5] "Educating today's students to succeed in tomorrow's world."[6]

How does data help your school system fulfill its mission or vision? What are the effective uses of data that support student success, inform development of comprehensive and balanced instruction, and help prepare students for the future?

Articulate the ways in which your school system will use data, and how those uses support the school system mission and vision. The list of data uses doesn't have to be granular. In fact, broad strokes are best at this point. You may decide that the purposes for collecting student data are to administer the basic operations of the school system, to support student learning, improve classroom instruction and inform teachers, empower students in pursuing their goals, and inform parents about their child's progress. Whatever the uses, ensure that you can tie them in some way to your mission and vision. That becomes part of the lens through which future decisions about data will be made.

LEARN THE LAWS

Get clear on what laws apply to your school system and understand the requirements. This will inform a good deal of the policy and process development you undertake. In addition to FERPA, PPRA, COPPA, and CIPA, what are the state student data privacy laws that apply? Also consider any requirements of your state education code, reporting, and records retention requirements.

Reading laws is not always easy or enjoyable for everyone. They are complex, sometimes conflict, and reading them is rarely sufficient to then be able to extrapolate how to implement them. There are nuances, best practices and history of implementation and enforcement that provide that clarity.

A good, basic starting point for many of the concepts behind privacy laws is the Fair Information Practice Principles (FIPPS). These principles were developed in the 1970s, and whether by design or by accident, FIPPS form the basis for almost every privacy law written. The specific listing of FIPPs can vary depending on the source, but the concepts are near universal. They are relatively simple to understand, and can serve as a guide to begin thinking about how to manage data privacy responsibilities. The FIPPS concepts are as follows:

- *Transparency*: provide clear notice to individuals about what personally identifiable information is collected, used, shared, and maintained.

- *Individual Participation*: ensure that individuals are able to review, copy, and correct or amend their personal information; information should be collected with consent or knowledge of the individual.
- *Purpose Specification*: articulate the authority that permits collection of personal information and the purposes for which it is intended to be used.
- *Data Minimization*: collect only personal information that is directly relevant and necessary for the specified purpose; use and disclose it only as necessary to fulfill the purpose for which it was collected; retain it only for as long as is necessary to fulfill that purpose.
- *Use Limitation*: use personal information only for the specified purpose for which it was collected and for no other purpose.
- *Data Quality and Integrity*: ensure that personal information remains accurate, timely, relevant, and complete.
- *Security*: protect personal information through appropriately reasonable security standards against risks such as loss, unauthorized access or use, destruction, modification, or unintended or inappropriate disclosure.
- *Accountability and Auditing*: be accountable for compliance with these principles, provide training to all individuals who use the personal information, and audit the use of personal information to demonstrate compliance with the relevant privacy protection requirements.

You may recognize many of the FIPPS concepts in FERPA, PPRA, COPPA, and other data privacy laws. Understanding FIPPS provides a foundation for understanding ideas in many of the privacy laws, and for informing your data privacy compliance policies. You may also consider developing data privacy compliance program goals to match each of the principles.

However, understanding FIPPS is not a substitute for learning the laws. Short of taking an immersive law course on each of the regulations, do refresh your understanding of the laws enough to be fluent in the basic requirements. Remember that the federal laws are not new. FERPA and PPRA were enacted in the 1970s, predating technology as it's used in the classroom today. CIPA and COPPA were enacted in 2000, with the most recent updates for any of the laws available for review since 2012. As such, there should be some basic fluency and protections that have been in place in the school system that predate technology. If you are not up to speed on the requirements, try to identify someone in the school system who is.

There is always the potential for laws to be updated, clarified, or rewritten, so now that you're working on a school system compliance program, monitor regulatory activity to stay abreast of changes at the federal and state level. Learning about any new regulations as they're being developed will help you keep your program a step ahead of future changes.

There are also a variety of credible free resources that can supplement your reading.[7] Then engage with competent privacy counsel or a compliance expert for deeper guidance and training.

Resources are often cited as a reason why school systems don't have access to qualified counsel or compliance experts. Don't shy away from the problem; instead, get creative and tackle it head on. Identify who it is you would like to engage with, or your top five options. Look for someone with deep expertise in student data privacy. Then ask: What would it take and what would it cost? Can you pool resources with other school systems or get support at discounted rates? There are also a number of qualified experts, including attorneys at top-tier law firms, with deep privacy expertise who may be willing to, and are often required to, provide a certain amount of pro bono support every year. Why couldn't that be for you?

The point is that the doors won't open if no one knows what you need.

Network with other school systems in your state to learn how they've tackled the problem, and connect with your state board of education for any additional free resources they can provide related to implementing the laws properly. Identify conferences, workshops, webinars, and other free to low-cost events in your local area. If you can't find any, ask the attorneys and compliance experts when you reach out to them. If they can't make their services cost-effective for you, they will certainly have a large network of other experts, so they may be able to recommend someone who can.

UNDERSTAND COMMUNITY EXPECTATIONS

Just because something is legal doesn't mean that it's going to be acceptable in your community. Parents and students may not be comfortable with certain uses of data that are permitted by federal and state laws. Understanding how your community stakeholders view the utility of student data also helps to inform the policies you will ultimately create for your school system.

If you hear from parents on a regular basis about technology and data privacy, you may already have a good handle on their expectations and reservations. Commonly asked questions will alert you to some of their more pressing concerns.

If you don't hear from parents about technology and data use, why not? Is it because they are already well informed about your practices and are comfortable with them? Is your data privacy compliance program robust and well understood? Is data privacy less of a concern because of other, more serious issues facing parents in the community? Is there normally low engagement from parents in your school system?

In some communities, school systems need to focus resources for engaging with parents on other fundamentals, such as ensuring that they have the proper paperwork for vaccinations and free and reduced lunch applications. In other communities, parents are early adopters of technology, and the positive results they see with their child gives them a sense of comfort regarding the school system's technology and data privacy programs. Still others see a combination of these issues, or there are other serious issues that must take precedence over privacy.

If parents in your community are not engaged around data privacy issues, do you know why, and do you have a good grasp on how they would view your intended uses of student personal information?

If not, consider whether or not it would be appropriate to conduct outreach to pressure-test your intended uses of data in alignment with your school mission and vision. If that's not possible, look to other community values and norms for a sense of what types of data use would be most palatable in your area.

BUILD THE BOUNDARIES

With the school system mission and vision, intended uses of data, the restrictions and obligations of the laws, and the community standards in hand, it is time to incorporate any additional school system requirements for general use of student personal information. Are there existing ethics policies or codes of conduct that must also be considered, or specific expectations regarding outcomes for the program that must be met in any given school

Figure 6.1   Establishing Compliance Norms.

year that are relevant to how the school system will protect the privacy of student data?

Leadership should help define any ethical boundaries for the school system, taking into consideration local expectations, comfort with technology and data use, existing policies, and the laws. Leadership can also help define what is feasible in terms of resources available to protect student data. This in turn can further inform what volume of data and technology provider relationships a school system is capable of managing properly. Figure 6.1 illustrates some of the many considerations for establishing your compliance norms.

Compliance Mission, Goals, and Metrics

Create a mission statement for the compliance program that incorporates why the school system collects student data and how it will use data to support the broader school system mission. Also establish the purpose for the compliance program and the overarching goals.

Document who will run the data privacy compliance program, who will be responsible for enforcement and decision making, how the program will be resourced, and how leadership will engage on maintaining the integrity and accountability of the program.

Finally, propose the first set of goals for the program and the time frame for completion. Establish a roadmap for achievement and success, then get ready to do the work.

Chapter 7

Preparing for a Data Privacy Impact Assessment

To identify which current school system practices need to change in order to align with the mission and meet the compliance goals, or sometimes even simply understand where to begin building a compliance program, you need to establish benchmarks around existing data collection, handling, storage, use, disclosure, and deletion policies and practices, as well as those of your technology providers. This includes understanding what employees know about the requirements, how well existing policies and processes are followed, and your controls over student personal information when it's shared with third parties.

A preassessment can be a useful tool in establishing benchmarks and determining where to focus energies in the opening phase of the compliance program work.

If you already have a mature compliance program in place and you have engaged in annual review of the policies, practices and systems, a preassessment may not be necessary. You may already know, based on facts in hand, where the risks are most pressing or where the policies and processes have not been reviewed regularly. If that's the case, you may choose to skip the preassessment and go right to the full assessment.

However, even with a mature compliance program, a preassessment is informative if you need to identify where to focus your energies or where improvement will be most impactful. In addition, if you plan to make significant changes to a system that stores student personal information or a process for handling that information, a preassessment of the planned changes will reveal whether or not your future plans will have an adverse impact on existing privacy protections.

The preassessment, or threshold assessment, identifies current practices and areas of the data protection efforts that appear to be out of alignment. For example, a preassessment may reveal where practices do not match up with existing policies and processes, if data is not adequately protected, or where employees are not being trained properly. Those results then identify where a full privacy impact assessment is needed to dig more deeply and reveal the extent of any concerns.

A preassessment can also provide reassurance that things seem to be operating as expected and as needed. If that is the case, you may wish to conduct a full assessment at a later date for auditing purposes, but you can do so with reassurance that there are no apparent burning issues in that area that need to be prioritized. This allows you to conserve resources and move focus to another area, until you identify the project that seems to be most blatantly out of alignment with expectations.

The preassessment usually consists of a series of questions, asked of a team that is responsible for a system, policy, or process. The questions are designed to elicit information about how the individuals who operate and access the system follow a policy or implement a process actually function, and whether or not actions match up with the words on paper. The preassessment can also be done to assess whether or not behavior matches up with the requirements of the laws.

To ensure that the preassessment is successful, begin by defining the scope of the work. You may choose to review a system, a data set, a policy, or a process. There are numerous options on this front. To help narrow it down and prioritize the order in which items should be assessed, consider existing knowledge, resources, and the complexity of each item. If this is the first assessment of this type for the school system, beginning the process with a relatively straightforward task will help build positive reinforcement and momentum for the program.

For example, you might choose to start by simply reviewing the annual FERPA notice against the legal requirements, and how the school system ensures that it is sent to all parents with students enrolled in the school system. A small but important policy and procedure review is actually a great place to start getting experience with the work, and can set the state for bigger accomplishments in the future.

Sample Subjects for Preassessment

These are just some of the potential topics for a preassessment or threshold assessment. The results of that work will determine whether or not the item should be subject to a full privacy impact assessment.

- justification or need for each data element collected by the school system
- required annual FERPA notice to parents, the directory information notice, and how responses are managed
- who has access to student personal information, for what purpose, and procedures for granting and revoking access permissions
- who has access to what data storage systems, for what purpose, and procedures for granting and revoking access permissions
- rules for sharing student personal information among employees
- where data is stored (internally or externally, system, country)
- how long data is retained
- security incident response procedure and training
- disaster recovery procedures and testing
- assessment of procured technology provider products and services
- assessment of technology provider products and services brought into the classroom by teachers
- quality, efficacy, scope, and timeliness of existing employee training
- protocols for securing data in transit
- protocols for securing data at rest
- procedures for accessing student personal information, including system authentication requirements
- password complexity and change rules
- policies regarding where data may be stored
- policies governing use of personal devices and how data may be accessed remotely
- rules for communications related to privacy and security
- website privacy and security policies

IDENTIFY STAKEHOLDERS

In order to conduct a preassessment, you must first identify the relevant stakeholders. Stakeholders generally include those with ownership and decision-making responsibility for a data system, data set, or procedure; individuals who manage daily operations; and those who use the data. Stakeholders might include

- system operators;
- security, engineering, and development personnel;
- data set users; and/or
- applicable or involved third parties.

Not all stakeholders will be involved in the preassessment; however, identifying and considering the full set of stakeholders helps to ensure that no critical perspectives are left out.

The data subjects are stakeholders as well; however, given the complexity and technical nature of the operation, as well as the goal of revealing gaps and risks, it would be rather unusual, and possibly legally unpalatable, to include them in the compliance preassessment or assessment.

Instead, ensure that the questions you ask in the preassessment take into consideration the community norms and values you have already explored, as well as any pressing parent concerns. Later on, once you have mitigated risk and developed new policies and procedures, you may go back to the community to present and explain how and why you changed the way the school system operates around a particular issue. Community feedback at that stage will help to inform future, ongoing improvements in the compliance program.

WRITE THE QUESTIONNAIRE

Develop a survey instrument for the preassessment. It may be a simple pencil-and-paper questionnaire, an online survey, or a spreadsheet of questions cross-referenced by applicable teams. Remember, this is about assessing where you need to begin the compliance work. It's about gaining valuable insight into whether or not stakeholders are fluent in and are following current policies and processes, and whether or not current policies and processes in a particular area of operation are sufficient to protect the privacy of student personal information, or at least are not high risk.

It is not about singling out any individual (unless you choose to add a human resources and individual training component to the work), so ideally, answers will be collected anonymously, perhaps categorized only by team, function, or stakeholder group.

Consider questions that will help to elicit whether or not stakeholders have been provided with the information, training, and guidance they need to execute in alignment with any existing policies or otherwise in compliance with the laws. As an example, questions that might be asked in a preassessment focused on protection of student personal information in and out of a key system might include the following:

- What system is the student personal information stored in and how does that system operate?
- Where is the system located?
- Where and from whom is the data collected?
- Is the data uploaded automatically into the system, or is it uploaded manually?
- Who is responsible for the data upload process, and how are they trained on secure upload practices and held accountable?
- Does data move out of the system, and if so, to where?
- What is the data used for?
- With whom is it shared?
- Who has access to the system and the data?
- How is the system secured?
- When and how is the data deleted?
- What is the process for granting and revoking access?
- How are access records used, changed, disclosed and secured?
- Are there any third parties operating in connection with the system? If so, how have their privacy and security practices been assessed, and how is the school system maintaining direct control over the data?
- Who is able to provide third parties with access to the data?
- How is data received by third parties limited and controlled?
- Is there a disaster recovery plan in place for the system? When was it tested and what were the results?
- Was a security audit, penetration test, and vulnerability scan conducted? If so, what were the results?

Also collect all documented policies and process applicable to the system.

Review the documented policies and processes in relation to the laws, the school system mission and vision, community norms and expectations, and any additional policies or requirements that have been provided by leadership. Are there gaps? Do the policies and procedures hold up under this scrutiny?

Next, turn your attention to the responses to the questionnaire. Compare the answers with the documented policies and processes. Do they match? Are there areas of discrepancy between what is expected as noted in a policy or process and the actual practice as noted in the results to the questionnaire? Do the answers reflect a base of knowledge that you would expect from someone operating or accessing the system or data in question?

If you are planning changes to the system, would the existing policies, processes, and behaviors be sufficient to protect the student personal information even with the changes? Are there fundamental issues about how people are operating that may need to be addressed before implementing any changes?

Depending on the results, you may determine that this particular system, policy, or process is operating as expected and as required.

Conversely, you may determine that there are critical issues that could adversely impact the privacy of student data. If you are considering changes to a system, the preassessment may reveal that the changes will adversely impact existing data protections. In either of these cases, the next step would be to move to a full privacy impact assessment.

If you conduct a number of preassessments and end up with an equal number that are likely good candidates for a full assessment, engage in a form of triage to determine what to tackle first. Consider the apparent risk to student personal information, and use your best judgment to prioritize what to move ahead with first.

Since you will not have a complete picture of the issues based on a preassessment, you may need to interview stakeholders to let them know what you've found in the results and why it appears to be a pressing concern. They may be able to propose simple solutions or interim solutions that will mitigate the risk until a full assessment can be conducted.

Chapter 8

First Steps in the Data Privacy Impact Assessment

You may choose to preassess if you find it helpful in benchmarking and prioritizing where to conduct a full assessment. If you have conducted preassessments, you will have identified the specific areas of your data-handling practices that are good candidates for a full privacy impact assessment.

However, you know your school system best, and may choose to just skip the preliminaries and head straight for the full assessment. If you have existing benchmarks, if you know where your biggest risks are, or if the idea of doing preassessments across the organization is simply too daunting, you're a good candidate to start with a full assessment. Just be sure that as you do it, you record benchmarks as well as gaps.

The privacy impact assessment is used to identify and then minimize the risks to personal information. It may be conducted on the entire organization's data privacy practices, or on a particular system, a small data set, or a specific segment of the data-handling operations, such as one that you've identified as being at risk in a preassessment.

The approach described here uses the example of assessing the entire organization's practices for protecting the privacy of all student personal information. It begins with the whole data set and moves outward to the systems, uses, stakeholders, and all of the individual components that make up the data privacy and security controls. It provides a more holistic assessment of the privacy practices at large. From there, you can trace the data to all the separate projects, systems, policies, processes, and individuals whose behavior impacts the privacy of the data. However, if you are conducting an assessment of a particular policy, process, or system, the steps are essentially the same. Just apply the steps here and in the next few chapters to the particular project you want to focus on.

IDENTIFY STAKEHOLDERS

As with the preassessment, the privacy impact assessment requires enlistment of key stakeholders. Keep in mind that the privacy impact assessment is initially focused on data and systems, and later on policy and process. That may help determine who is at the table during different stages of the work.

Typical stakeholders to lead this work would be the chief privacy officer or chief compliance officer who oversees the project and privacy-related compliance policy development, a chief technology officer or chief information officer who will manage data and system mapping, and a chief security officer to oversee establishment and implementation of security standards and requirements, including security policies, in collaboration with the privacy lead. These are not soloed efforts, as the work is synergistic. Stakeholders should work collaboratively, leveraging each other's expertise in different subject matter.

You will be gathering information from different corners of the school system, so you may wish to assign owners to different elements of the project. These individuals will be responsible for gathering information related to their work or area of expertise. This type of "divide and conquer" project management will make the work more efficient and certainly easier than having one individual be single-handedly responsible for collecting the required materials.

As you go through the work, you may also find it most efficient if stakeholders complete portions of the assessment on their own and report back results, or you may find it helpful to work in a collaboration all the way through. Much may depend on the size of your school system, the number of stakeholders, and available expertise.

Although you may not have a robust and formal compliance program, gather any existing policies and procedures related to data collection, handling, use, access, retention, security, and legal compliance. Also gather any existing data and system maps.

Collect annually required legal notices and student-survey instruments, any documented procedures for providing parents, and any eligible students with access to the student education record, as well as the procedure for those individuals to request amendment and correction of information in the record. You'll come back to this material later in the process.

Make a list of all the types of personal information the school system collects from or about students. This includes names, ID numbers, grade level, grades, test scores, behavior, health information, parent information, custodial relationships, addresses, sports teams, clubs, counseling appointments, attendance, tardiness, individualized learning plans, career goals, awards, demerits, photos, videos, parent notes, and more. Try to capture a list of every data element. Make the list as exhaustive as possible.

As you can imagine, it will likely take a team to get this done.

EVALUATE THE COLLECTION

Why do you collect each item of student personal information that you've listed? From whom do you collect it? Is each necessary? Why? How is each data element used? Is that use serving the educational purpose and operational needs of the school system? Is it required for state reporting? Each data element should have a legal, justifiable purpose.

Categorize the data according to a small number of broad use cases, such as

- state requirements;
- school operations;
- student support (academic); and
- student support (nonacademic).

Can you articulate the requirement or use case for each data element? If you have any for which you cannot provide a justification, consider why the data is collected and what the implications would be if it was no longer collected. If, after consulting with all possible users of the data, you can find no adverse impacts if the school system no longer collected that data element, you may propose that the data be destroyed and collection be discontinued.

Create a Classification Scheme

Armed with a list of the personal information you have from and about students, and a reason for having each data element on hand, the next step is to develop a classification scheme so the data can be sorted into categories based on level of sensitivity of the data, and potential for harm to the individual or the school system if a security incident results in unauthorized release of or access to the information. Usually this involves creating just a small number of categories.

In the example below, the categories are created with naming conventions ("public," "restricted," or "sensitive") that illustrate the sensitivity of the data, and risk levels indicating the potential for harm in the event that there is unauthorized access to that data.

- Public with Authorization: Low Risk
- Restricted Access: Medium Risk
- Sensitive Information: High Risk

Create a description for each category to further define the risk and illustrate with examples. Here are some possible definitions:

- *Public with Authorization: Low Risk.* Data in this category is not made public without an authorized reason or request. However, this category consists of only data elements that could be made available publicly without harm or risk to the data subject. Directory information should meet the requirements of this category.
- *Restricted Access: Medium Risk.* Consists of data elements necessary for employees to perform their duties; however, not every employee requires or should have access to all data in this category. Access must be assigned and controlled. In the event of unauthorized access or release of the data, resulting harm might include embarrassment, upset, or community outcry. There is no financial, identity, or other anticipated harm from unauthorized access to this data.
- *Sensitive Information: High Risk.* Consists of data elements available only to select individuals, usually at the administration level. Data in this category poses the highest risks to the individual and to the school system if released to an unauthorized actor. Resulting harm might include

embarrassment, mental or emotional duress, community outcry, and more significant personal and legal repercussions, including financial risk, fraud, and identity theft.

When developing your definitions, it can be instructive to consult your state data breach law to determine what would trigger required notification in the event of unauthorized access.

Depending on the scope of the data on hand, you may choose to use only three categories, or you may add an extra category if necessary. Whatever scheme you use, keep the categories as simple and manageable as possible. More than four categories can start to get unwieldy and create unnecessary complexity as the process unfolds.

Classify the Data

When the data categories have been defined, go back to the data list and place each data element in the appropriate category.

The sensitive, or high-risk, category is often the easiest one to complete. This category includes data elements that have strong potential to cause harm to the individual or to the school system if the data is released. Examples include a national identifier such as a Social Security number or tax ID number, fingerprints, passwords, electronic or other ID numbers that can be used to gain access to financial information, actual financial information, and similarly sensitive information.

The public, or low-risk, category might include student names, grade levels, and ages. Consider the information that you have previously determined to be directory information under FERPA. There will be instances in which a school system might classify a data element as directory information but is comfortable releasing that information publicly only under certain circumstances.

For example, a student's photo, height, and weight might be directory information for the purpose of publishing the roster for a sports team, but when engaged in the exercise of classifying data, there may be discomfort labeling this as "low-risk" or "public" information. Keep in mind that classifying the data is not necessarily dependent on which authorized individuals will see it or the specific purpose for which it will be shared. Classifying data as "public" does not mean it will be shared widely or without an authorized

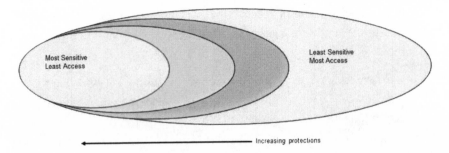

Most Sensitive
Least Access

Least Sensitive
Most Access

Increasing protections

Figure 8.1

request. Instead, for the purpose of this exercise, place each data element in the proper category depending on the risk of harm to the individual if it were accessed by an *unauthorized* actor.

It is understood that combinations of low-risk data may render the data to be more sensitive than each data element standing alone. That potential will be addressed at a later point, in the discussion regarding disclosure of information.

Restricted information, or information categorized as "medium risk," is often the category that provokes the most questions and challenges. It is also often the reason why many end up with four or more categories of data instead of three. The important thing is that there should be clear distinctions in the risk level between the categories, and that within a category, the data should share common attributes related to the risk profile if it were subject to unauthorized access.

Once the data has been classified, you'll begin to develop the policies, procedures, and practices that will apply to each category to keep it private and protected. Figure 8.1 illustrates how data sensitivity, access, and levels of protection around data might begin to unfold.

Data Minimization

If it's not apparent yet, as you go through the data classification exercise you'll find that each category of data requires a different level of security in order to keep it protected from unauthorized access or unintentional release. Before determining the security level for each data category based on the data elements in each category, assess the data list in light of a fundamental privacy and security concept: data minimization.

You've already conducted one data minimization exercise when you established a justification for collection of each data element. Now take each category and do a thorough review with an eye toward answering two questions:

1. Even though you have a justifiable reason for having this data element, do you need it?
2. What is the impact on the school system if you no longer collected this data?

If the answers are "no" and "none," your next data privacy compliance project might very well be to do a discovery exercise to determine where all of that data is stored and take steps to securely delete it from the primary and backup systems.

The most likely candidate for deletion is the Social Security number. This is often the most valuable piece of student information held by school systems. It is sensitive by any definition, high risk, and an attractive target for hackers and thieves. Many school systems have moved away from collecting the social security number as a form of ID, and some states have banned the practice.

If your school system can operate without collecting student Social Security numbers, do it. Make this the first documented policy of your compliance program.

Identity theft of children is a very real threat. It is a "clean" ID, with no debt or other credit record associated with it, and can easily be used to create a new identity. That theft may remain undetected for years. Often it's not discovered until the child grows up and begins to open their own financial accounts or lines of credit. Since it is so valuable to the criminal set, it is an attractive target, and school systems are a known repository for student Social Security numbers.

Carefully review the state data retention laws to determine exactly what data fields the school system does and does not need to retain. Chances are that, with some exceptions, the Social Security number is not a required data element for data retention. If that is the case in your state, stop collecting student Social Security numbers and delete the ones you have on hand.

Go back into the archives as far as you can to delete the data field wherever it exists in the records. (Possibly the only thing worse than someone gaining unauthorized access to a current student's Social Security number is someone gaining unauthorized access to a former student's Social Security number when that student left your school system twenty or thirty years ago and no longer has any expectation that the school system is still retaining that information, and when there has been no legal requirement for it to have been retained.)

While you are looking at the state data retention requirements, make a list of all student personal information data elements that you are not required to retain once students have left the school system. In the world of data privacy, when data is no longer needed, it should be deleted.

Identifying and securely deleting data you are not required to retain is your next data privacy compliance project. Documenting what data that, as a rule, you will no longer collect, can be your first data privacy compliance policy.

Data minimization is not only a positive privacy win for the student, but it is also a mitigating factor for the school system's risk profile. The less data you have on hand, the less there is to protect. Sensitive data presents potential liability issues in the event of unauthorized access and can be prohibitively expensive to protect. The best protection is to not have collected it.

Chapter 9

Security

Whatever data you do have on hand needs to be protected from unauthorized access. With your data neatly classified according to sensitivity and risk, and any extraneous data on the road to being deleted, the next logical focus is security. You may choose to protect all categories of data with one strong data security standard, appropriate to protecting the highest-sensitivity data. On the other hand, you may choose to protect the data in alignment with different security standards, based on the sensitivity of the data.

The path you choose may depend in large part on existing systems and how and where the data must be stored, accessed, and moved. Either way, it is still important to establish the minimum security protocols that your school system will *require* for each data category. Even if you find that your server meets the security requirements for each category of data, your systems may change in the future. In addition, you need to inform your technology providers of any security requirements you have for the categories of data that you may share.

While you may choose to protect student first names with the same security standards that you do a password, your technology providers may not be able to do the same. Established standards allow you to communicate strong and reasonable protection requirements to those who wish to do business with your school system, with appropriate flexibility where needed and acceptable.

Start with your internal protections. Examine each category of data and determine baseline physical, technical, and administrative security requirements. The requirements should be based on reasonable industry standards appropriate to the sensitivity of the data and the risk profile.

What technical measures should be in place? Determine the proper and current standards for encryption of data in transit, and what data elements need to be encrypted at rest. Where will encryption keys be stored? Who will manage them and how will their access be audited? What are the right firewall settings for a system with sensitive data? Does your system allow for segmented access, such that access to one area of the system with low-risk data doesn't automatically grant access to an area of the system with sensitive data?

Be mindful of physical safeguards as well. How will access to the servers be controlled? Who will have credentials to access server areas, and how complex will those credentials be? Will you make use of locks, passkeys, cameras, or other devices to monitor access? How will data on paper be stored?

What policies and procedures are in place to monitor systems for threats, authorize and document code changes, and implement checks and balances to ensure that the required security protocols are followed?

DATA ACCESS

Access to personal information is a great example of where data privacy and data security disciplines overlap in complementary and supportive ways. This is an area of data protection that involves all of the employees who have access to student personal information. If the school system has been too permissive in allowing employees access to data, it can also be one of the most challenging to address, since it may require that you revoke data access from some employees, often an unpopular but necessary change.

FERPA requires that student personally identifiable information be disclosed to those with "legitimate educational interests." The first question then is, who in the school system has a legitimate educational interest in what data?

No one should have access to student personal information unless it is required for them to do their job, and then they should have access to only that set of necessary information and no more. This is usually accomplished by establishing "rule/role-based" access policies, whereby a set of rules for data access is created providing only the data necessary for each role.

Start with a world where no one in the school system has access to any student data. Are you breathing a little easier at the thought of that? Feels like the data is safer already, doesn't it? That's often because human error is to blame in a good deal of data security incidents, and once access to data is provided, it is up to each individual to maintain or hinder the security of that data and the privacy of the data subject. The wider the distribution of data, the more challenging it is to maintain privacy and security protections.

However, it is possible to implement consistent privacy and security protections. It just takes planning, policy, process, training, and controls.

Starting with a baseline of "no one has access," create a list of all the teams in your school system. This likely includes a variety of administrator roles, support staff, teachers, athletic coaches, guidance counselors, curriculum instructors, education specialists, librarians, substitute teachers, technology specialists, and more. Map data elements to each job category, and note where the access should be limited to the students served or supported by the individuals on that team.

For example, a principal may have access to all the student personal information in the school. A classroom teacher may have access to the student personal information only for the students under that teacher's supervision. However, even then the teacher may not require access to all of that student's personal information.

Teachers do need access to a good deal of information about their students: names, ages, grade level, grades, test scores, aptitudes, attitudes, behaviors, perhaps health risks, the custodial parent, and more. However, there are also decisions to be made about some of the data. For example, do teachers in your school need access to everything about the student? If a child had a minor behavioral issue or falied a subject in third grade and has performed well since then, does their eighth-grade teacher need that information?

Many of these decisions will be dependent on how your data systems are set up, how the data tables are structured, and whether or not access can be granted to only limited data elements on each individual student. The decisions will also be dependent on the school system structure. Some school systems may have specialists handling different aspects of student support, while other school systems may have employees who are generalists, handling a wide array of duties to support the students. These individuals may need access to more data about each student they support than do others.

Overall, however, the idea is to grant data access that is necessary, but not to overshare. Be sure that the decisions you make regarding who may access what data are in alignment with the laws, and document the decisions about who is authorized to access what types of data.

Also consider the logging capabilities of your systems. Are you able to determine who logged into which system, what was viewed, accessed, downloaded, or changed in the system? Are the logs date and time stamped? Are they recorded and reviewed, or accessible if necessary, such as in the event of a data security incident? This type of visibility can also be helpful in supporting a more fluid rule/role based access program.

It also can be particularly useful if your data system is not configurable with logical separations or customizable to assign field-level permissions to individuals. In that case, at the least, you can maintain an audit trail of activity to rely on to document that there was no unauthorized or unwarranted data access until the systems catch up with your access requirements.

If you find this task to be rather daunting, a relatively simple place to start is with the high-risk category of data. That is because very few roles require access to this information, so making decisions around it should be more straightforward. With a few decisions in hand, you'll have momentum to keep going.

Rule/Role-Based Access Policy

Now that you know who may have access to what data, you are ready to document those rules as policy. This policy needs to be accompanied by a procedure that details how the policy will be implemented. The policy may include

- the circumstances under which an employee will be granted access to student personal information;
- the minimum required information each employee will be granted in order to perform their role, including what data or categories of data are included;
- that access credentials must be revoked when an employee changes roles or leaves the school system; and
- detail about who enforces the policy and makes decisions about rule/role-based access, and how often compliance must be monitored.

The procedure may include details about

- how employees obtain access to data;
- who is responsible for tracking system access, and how the records are maintained;
- how access is revoked when an employee leaves employment or changes job roles, and how those records are maintained;
- what type of credentials are required to access each system;
- how complex must they be, how often must they change, and how those rules are enforced;
- how employees can securely store their access credentials and how storage rules are enforced; and
- how compliance is monitored, including any reporting requirements.

Before you put pen to paper, review the chapter on writing policies to help ensure the policy rollout is successful.

It is prudent to review the data classification and associated rules at least once each year and examine whether or not the security standards you assigned to each category are still valid and appropriate. They may need to be upgraded as technology evolves, data-use cases change, or school system organization changes.

After some experience working with the classification system, you may decide that there are one or two data elements that really belong in a higher category. However, that does not need to involve repeating this entire exercise if it was managed well, thoughtfully, and with attention to the entire student data ecosystem the first time around. Simply move the data to the more appropriate category, and ensure that it is protected at the same level as all other information in that category. Document the changes and the rationale behind them, including who authorized the changes and when they were made.

ASSESSING AND IMPLEMENTING REASONABLE SECURITY

This is not a security text, so we won't delve into specific security requirements or the complexities of network security. However, it is helpful to have an understanding of some of the basics that make up "reasonable security."

Most privacy laws require implementation of security as part of the ecosystem around data protection. In the United States, that commonly takes the form of a requirement to implement "reasonable security." However, "reasonable security" is not defined, and the laws tend to avoid being prescriptive in this area.

There are a few reasons for the absence of specificity. One is that implementing strong security is often dependent on technology. However, technology is constantly evolving. In addition, bad actors get more sophisticated in their tactics and abilities, and technological protections need to evolve to remain a step ahead. For example, a reasonable encryption standard today may not afford the same strong protections in the future. Being specific about the technology means the prescription must be updated over time, which is not easy when that prescription is baked into a law.

In addition, what is a reasonable protection for one type of data may not be reasonable for another. It may be more than reasonable to protect a first name with access controls, limits on who may access the data, and by ensuring that it remains separated from more sensitive data. It would be unreasonable to protect a Social Security number with only those protections.

The reasonableness of data security is often dependent on the nature of the information being protected.

However, there are a variety of industry standards that provide excellent guidance on reasonably appropriate security protocols. In addition, the FTC does provide a starting point for understanding the fundamentals of reasonable security from a regulatory perspective.[1] They include some of the FIPPS concepts, illustrating how privacy and security work together, as well as a few specifics to keep in mind, summarized here for school systems.

First, don't collect data you don't need, use data only for the purpose for which it was collected, and delete data when no longer needed.

Make data available only to those individuals who require access in order to perform their function. Teachers don't need to see information on every student in the school, only those students in their particular classroom. The same thing goes for coaches, guidance counselors, and other school employees.

Restrict system access credentials so that only those with the authority and responsibility to access data in production systems and change those systems have the ability to do so.

Require complex, unique passwords in accordance with existing industry standards. This can be particularly challenging for school systems, where a variety of individuals need to maintain access to different systems. There is often a culture of permitting overly simplistic passwords and for employees to maintain those passwords posted on their desks. That behavior must change. Passwords need to be appropriately complex, stored securely, and ideally unique to each system.

Implement protocols to protect against brute force attacks. Lock individuals out after repeated login attempts. Test authentication protocols for known vulnerabilities and protect accordingly.

Encrypt sensitive information in transit and at rest, using current, valid encryption standards configured properly. Don't forget to consider appropriate security protocols for protecting data in all media, including paper, portable drives, and shared services.

Use standard methods such as firewalls and network segmentation to prevent unauthorized access to your systems, and monitor activity for threats and vulnerabilities.

Require use of VPN if employees are permitted to access school systems from home or other environments. Do not allow access from unsecured Wi-Fi, and require certain minimum standards of security on personal devices that will be used to access the school system network. This should include antivirus software and firewalls. If employees do not require remote access in order to conduct their work, do not permit it.

Provide training in industry standard secure coding practices for engineers and other employees responsible for software development, if applicable. Ensure that teams carefully follow implementation requirements for any third-party technology configurations.

Audit and test security practices on an annual basis, and require that your technology providers are doing the same. Require that technology providers also implement reasonable security, appropriate to the data they receive, and ensure that commercially reasonable security in accordance with industry standards is a minimum contractual obligation.

Patch and update regularly and routinely, and implement threat monitoring of the network. Monitor official sources as well, to stay informed about potential issues.

Ensure that data is disposed of securely. That includes disposal of portable data devices and paper. A box of paper sitting out waiting to be picked up for shredding is just as vulnerable to theft as a laptop left in the backseat of a car.

Consider the entire ecosystem of data, where it is stored, where it travels, where it may be shared, and in what media format. Make it a goal to implement end-to-end reasonable security across all school system data.

For more information, consult the industry standards[2] along with a qualified data security expert and legal counsel for help in establishing what is the legally required "reasonable security," sufficient and appropriate to the data on hand.

Chapter 10

Disclosure, Deletion,
and Deidentification

At this point, you should know what data is being collected, the relative sensitivity of the data, who currently has access to the information and who should have access, and how the data should be protected. It's now time to document which student personal information you would consider sharing with parties outside of the school system, in accordance with the legal requirements, need, and the sensitivity of the data. You will likely work with a variety of technology providers. The personal information you share with them will vary widely.

A student information system (SIS) may be utilized for all of the student data. However, a tool that keeps track of student extracurricular activities or a system designed to support English language learners may not require, and therefore should not receive, the same volume and variety of data. Again, start with the personal information. What is required in order for the technology to work, and are there data elements or categories of data that you will deem too sensitive to disclose to technology providers?

With your data classification chart on hand, label the personal information data elements that the school system will not disclose to technology providers or other third parties. Are there data elements that are currently being shared that you would prefer to not share in the future? What would the implications be if you were to not share the data in the future, or if you were to revoke access from technology providers that currently have access to the data? Would that mean that certain technology products could no longer be used in the school system? If so, is that a tenable situation?

Recall that for the personal information you will disclose, it needs to remain protected in alignment with your established standards for the category. Also consider that when releasing certain personal information, it may result in low-risk elements being combined with high-risk elements. In those cases, the low-risk elements will need to be protected at higher standards if the data will remained combined. As you make decisions around data disclosure, document and codify them in your policies.

Deleting Data

Refer back to the review of your state's data-retention requirements for student education records. Which data elements must be maintained, and for how long? There will likely be data elements that need to be maintained for as long as the student is enrolled, and some that need to be maintained for years after the student has left the school system.

Create a policy in the form of a schedule for deleting unneeded student personal information when the student leaves the school system. Establish a process for how the deletion will be triggered and who will oversee the work to completion. Remember that these policies and processes also need to be documented. This documentation process is discussed in chapter 13.

With respect to data elements for which there is no state retention requirement, determine how long the school system will maintain those elements. Bear in mind that data is an asset and a liability. What you keep, you must protect, and protecting high volumes of sensitive data is an expensive proposition. Also consider what data elements need to be maintained attached to student personal information, and what may be maintained in deidentified form.

Data elements that need to be attached to student personal information should be only those required to support the student and comply with state requirements. There may be other data elements that are helpful to maintain because they are useful for research purposes and analytics that will reveal the efficacy of curriculum methods, behavioral interventions, graduation rates tied to course content or rigor, and related information that informs continuous school system improvement. All of this should be considered in determining what data you will keep, for how long, and whether or not it will be retained in identifiable or deidentified format. Table 10.1 illustrates how the different data rules may begin to take shape.

Wherever possible, deidentify the information and securely dispose of the student personal. Deidentified information is often sufficient for efficacy studies,

Table 10.1 Data Classification and Establishing Policy Requirements

Sensitive	Restricted	Public
Social Security numbers	Grades	Student names
Financial records	*Discipline records*	Athletic teams
Passwords	Classwork	Class photos
Health information	Attendance	Honors
...	Course rigor*	...
	Post-secondary plans*	
	...	

- Italics indicates data elements that will not be disclosed to a third party.
- Underlined indicates data elements that will be deleted when the student leaves the school system, if permissible under state law.
- Asterisk indicates data that will only be maintained in deidentified form when the student leaves the schools system.

forecasting, and even for longitudinal studies if the data can be coded properly. There will be instances in which student personal information must be retained, but when possible and practical, deidentify the data if it can't be deleted.

Recall that the FERPA standard for deidentifying data is broad and wide. It requires removal or obfuscation of all personally identifiable information, as well as a determination that the student is not personally identifiable through single or multiple release of information, considering all other reasonably available information, such as directory information that would have been subject to prior release.

Recall also, that while some data elements may not be personally identifiable on their own, they can identify an individual when combined with other data. Data about an individual that is "linked or linkable" to a student in a way that would allow "a reasonable person in the school community" without personal knowledge of the circumstances to identify the student with "reasonable certainty" is also considered to be personally identifiable information under FERPA, and so must be protected as such.

All the data must be considered, alone, in combination, in relation to a sample size in which it may be aggregated, in relation to the planned use case, in relation to other readily available data, and with consideration for the reasonable person standard.

Data deidentification is a complex process worthy of its own book. Consult a data scientist to develop a strict protocol consistent with the laws and established industry standards, and develop a careful review process before releasing reports or studies revealing deidentified data.

Chapter 11

Inventories and Making Maps

The work with the data is not done. Once you've managed to classify by risk, determined how the data should be secured, who should be permitted access to what data, how long data will be retained, what data will and will not be disclosed to any third parties, and what may be deidentified, it's time to look at how and where it moves.

The goal here is to have a visual representation or other documentation that establishes the flow of data into, within, and out of the school system. Where does each data element enter the school system, where is it stored, where is it transferred, and what are the access points? What systems house the data, and how are they connected to systems that the data moves to?

If you already have a technical schema for the systems, you're a step ahead. However, if the systems haven't been mapped, it can be a project for the future compliance roadmap. It's important documentation to maintain. It provides a quick visual benchmark of where data is stored and how it moves and is accordingly protected throughout its lifecycle. If you haven't created one yet, it need not slow you down in your initial assessment, especially if you don't have the resources to develop a technical diagram or data flow.

Instead, for initial purposes, create a very simple map. A hand-drawn illustration with boxes indicating systems and arrows demonstrating data movement can work just as well for the initial work as an elaborate process graphic, as long as it captures what data is stored where, and where it moves.

Compare the map to the existing decisions you've made about how each category of data should be protected. Is the data in systems that provide the appropriate levels of security protections? Is access to the systems appropriately restricted? Is the data encrypted at rest where needed and as it moves? Where it flows to third parties, are contracts in place to govern that data sharing and ensure that the data remains protected in accordance with the requirements you've established?

Your very simple map may grow in complexity as you go. Creating a complete map may take some time; however, it is a project worth doing as it is a very helpful reference document for the future. It creates a clear visual representation of the data that can be easily lined up against the newly established data protection protocols, access rules, as well as deletion schedules and policies about what may not be shared. It is also a helpful tool when it is time to audit the compliance program.

Before changing systems or bringing on new technology providers, the map can also be leveraged to ensure that the planned changes don't adversely impact protection of the data.

Identify Classroom Technologies

Another key piece of information for the privacy impact assessment is classroom technologies. The servers and administrative systems are usually brought in through a procurement process and managed by an IT team. That process should already involve a robust privacy and security assessment, and it is expected that these systems would also be assessed as part of the overall privacy impact assessment.

However, it is fairly common practice for teachers to bring free or low-cost websites, apps, and other connected products into the classroom without going through an administrative review or technology vetting process. A privacy impact assessment should shed light on what products and services have been brought into the classroom in this manner, so that the impact on data privacy can be considered.

Survey the teachers, librarians, and other instruction specialists who may be bringing apps, websites, and other connected products into the classroom. If possible, allow respondents to remain anonymous. As with the preassessment surveys, the goal at this point is simply to capture the information. Build a list as the results come in, and note where products are being used in multiple classrooms.

It should not surprise you to see results that reveal several hundred or more products being used across the classrooms. Rank them in order, based on the number of times they appear in survey results.

How many of the products were designed for use in the classroom? Are there any on the list that would be considered "general audience products," not specifically designed for use in education? If so, gather those into a separate list as they may be subject to additional scrutiny and policy development.

If the school system has a process that teachers are supposed to follow in order to have these products reviewed in advance, such as through a central vetting process, compare the lists you receive with the records on hand. Note whether or not products are being used that have not been vetted. This simple exercise should tell you if the vetting process is being followed or not.

If you do not have a vetting process for classroom technologies, guidance for establishing one will be discussed in chapter 14.

For now, it's time to face the truth about existing student data privacy protections.

Chapter 12

Gaps and Mitigation

Take what you've learned about the data, and the decisions you've made about how it should be protected, who should have access, how long it should be retained, and whether or not it should be shared, and see how that measures up against current practices.

Evaluate where the data is stored in relation to the physical, technical, and administrative security requirements that you established for each category of data. Leveraging that information and the data map, is there data stored in systems that do not meet the security thresholds appropriate to the sensitivity of the data stored within? Is it properly protected in transit between systems? Are the procedures for destroying data appropriately secure?

Are access and authentication protocols sufficiently complex for the nature of the systems and the data available?

Who has access to what data? Did you find that many more people in the organization have access to data than is ideal when considered from the perspective of rule/role-based access, where individuals are permitted access to only the data that is necessary in order for them to perform their jobs? Are teachers allowed access to data of students who are not in their classroom? Are athletic coaches permitted access to a health records system for all students, not just the students on sports teams whose health concerns are of a nature that it is necessary for the athletic coach to be aware?

Review the data deletion schedule that you created. How does that compare with current practices? Are data elements remaining on hand longer than is necessary?

What data has been shared with third parties, such as technology providers? Given the list of apps, websites, and other connected technologies that teachers have been bringing into the classrooms, do you know what data has been shared with whom? If you have a vetting process, has it been followed? What is the rate of compliance with the vetting process? Have records been kept of the data or types of data shared with technology providers? If so, does it match the requirements you've now established around what data the school system will and won't disclose?

POLICY AND NOTICE REVIEW

Review all of the policies and procedures that you collected at the start of the assessment. How do they align with the decisions you've made about how data should be managed? Do the documents accurately reflect the decisions you've made? Have you made decisions for which there was no corresponding, current document to compare against? Are there policies that should be in place that are not documented? Are there procedures that would be useful in guiding the teams about how data should be managed that are also not documented? Where are there legal requirements for which there is no accompanying policy or process?

Is there documentation of annual FERPA notices and directory information disclosures sent to the necessary parties? Do those notices meet the legal requirements?

Are there up-to-date records of third-party school officials, and the reasons for which they have access to any student personally identifiable information? Were parents and legal guardians informed of the legitimate education interest for which the school system designates a third party as a school official?

Create the Gap Report

By now, you likely have a good handle on where you have gaps that need to be addressed. Create a gap report in the form of a chart or table. For each policy, procedure, system, or practice you've reviewed, document the current state, the requirement based on the laws, district rules and community norms, and the next steps to achieve your objective based on any determinations you've made so far through the work you've conducted. Table 12.1 illustrates how you might consider structuring your gap report.

This is the beginning of the road to achieving compliance.

ADDRESS THE GAPS

After having established compliance benchmarks, looked at how student personal information is managed, and identified where actual practices are in relation to goals and requirements, it's time to create a plan to address the gaps.

There may be some gaps that can be eliminated and entirely corrected, but there is often some degree of risk that can be contained but not completely eliminated.

One thing that is certain is that there will be gaps to address. Everyone has gaps. Data protection is not perfect, and the work is never complete. It is an exercise in mitigating risk, being proactive about protecting the data, and constantly improving practices. The goal is to know what your gaps are and create a plan to address them. That will not happen all at once.

Resist the urge to become overwhelmed at this state. Some gaps will be more significant than others, and a line item on the gap report is not always indicative of a big remediation project ahead. Before you dive in, take the time to run a triage exercise on the gaps you have uncovered.

What Is the Risk?

There are a variety of risk types. Gaps may implicate risks that could result in

- regulatory action;
- litigation;
- reputational harm;
- parent mistrust;
- loss of insurance coverage;
- disqualification from bond applications;
- contractual breaches; and/or
- security incidents.

Table 12.1 Same Gap Report Template

POLICY OR PRACTICE	CURRENT STATE	REQUIREMENT	NEXT STEPS
ENCRYPTION OF DATA IN TRANSIT AND AT REST	Social Security numbers and passwords are encrypted in accordance with industry best practices; health information housed in system with outdated encryption standards.	All sensitive data must be encrypted in accordance with current, industry-standard best practices.	IT and security teams to assess feasibility of porting data to more secure system or upgrading current system standards.
DATA ACCESS	Athletic coaches have access to system that allows them to access sensitive data that has no bearing on their role or responsibilities.	Athletic coaches may have access only to student names, grades when they fall below the level required for eligibility on the team, and health information necessary to protect the safety of the student athlete.	Privacy officer to discuss the new requirement with the coaches and ensure that it meets the needs and doesn't jeopardize student academic or athletic performance or safety. IT to begin discovery on adjusting system permissions to restrict access.
ANNUAL FERPA NOTICE	A glitch in the system resulted in FERPA notices not being sent to parents in the third-grade class.	FERPA notice containing all the information required in the law must be sent annually to all parents.	Administration to send missing notices immediately. Engineers to develop roadmap for the necessary code fix. IT and privacy team to establish process for annual review of logs establishing that notices are sent properly in the future.

What is in the gap report that creates the most risk? What gap exists between a current practice and a legal requirement or a best practice for protecting the data that would have the most severe repercussions if the worst case scenario occurred? Is there an issue that is a violation of the law? Is there an issue that leaves sensitive data vulnerable to hackers? Could a lawsuit result from a current practice? Are there situations in which people may be upset, but would not result in tangible harm? Try to rank the risks in accordance with their severity.

Then consider the likelihood of that risk coming to fruition. The risk may be real, but which items are most likely to go wrong in the short term? Are there any gaps that, while not ideal, have an extremely small chance of actually causing a problem in the short term?

You may be able to establish a somewhat scientific and data-based approach to determining the likelihood of some of the risks to be realized. For others, it may not be possible to assign a factor of "potential to actually happen." There may even be an item or two for which you simply have a nagging feeling that they will be the ones that spark a crisis. (Don't ignore that feeling!)

Whether you use a data-based, well-researched approach to ranking the likelihood of realizing a risk, or you just want to put the ones that will keep you up at night at the top of the list, understand that if there are a number of items that are high risk, it may not be possible to fix all of them at once. If that is the case, as a next step, try to look at the likelihood of both the worst-case scenario occurring and the resources available to address items quickly.

Resources

Working on the gaps takes time, money, and energy. It is man hours not doing other work. It may mean that systems have to go down in order for things to be fixed. It may mean culture changes in an organization or significant adjustments to the ways in which people get their jobs done. The costs and the disruption need to be considered and factored into the decisions about what gaps to address when.

Some of the gaps, particularly those requiring security upgrades, may require additional budget. New systems may be needed, or additional development work may be required of the engineering team. Other issues may require training, or bringing in outside resources with subject matter expertise to support the work.

However, when dealing with privacy, it is also not uncommon to find that a number of the issues are human issues, not technology issues, implicating policy and process more than machines. This can be a good thing! It is sometimes easier to change code and configurations than it is to change behavior, but it is less expensive to address policies and processes than it is to fix machines.

Build Project Roadmaps

Decisions need to be made related to how to best balance risk, likelihood of the risk occurring, resources on hand to address the risk, and potential disruption to the school system while the risk is being addressed, in terms of system downtime, process change, and work on other priorities not being conducted. This requires discovery by the relevant teams.

Wherever possible, try to come up with different paths to resolve each gap, so that comparative cost-benefit and time-to-completion analysis of solutions can be assessed. Also assess the durability of proposed solutions over time. The aim is to develop solutions that will work within the school system for years to come, not ones that will need to be readdressed in the next year with a new policy, process, machine, or model.

Prioritize and schedule accordingly. Depending on the gaps, you may be looking at a multiyear project. That is not necessarily because the gaps are so significant. Sometimes it is simply that there are a number of small gaps, and the resources are not available to tackle everything at once. It may also be that some of the work is best scheduled for the summer months or winter breaks, in order to avoid disruption and ensure that the systems are working as expected before they need to handle the load of a busy workday.

Remember that each gap addressed, no matter how small, is a meaningful step in protecting the privacy of student data. It is, as they say, a marathon, not a sprint. Unless, of course, the gap is potentially disastrous. In that case, by all means sprint, but try to do it sensibly!

Assessment Report

Incorporate the project roadmap into the final gap report and package it for leadership. Ideally, the detailed gap report will be accompanied by an overview of the entire assessment, including an explanation of how it will improve the privacy posture of the school system.

Include findings, recommendations, and the remediation plan and deliver to the leadership team for review and for approval of the plans.

Are You Comfortable Being Uncomfortable?

Risk tolerance is not easy to quantify, but depending on the results of the assessment, and considering that it is challenging for any organization to address multiple issues at once, decisions often need to be made about the amount and type of risk the school system is willing to tolerate in the short term.

What repercussions, if they did come to fruition, is the school system prepared to manage? If the answer is "none," are there interim steps that can be taken to reduce the risk or the likelihood of the risk until resources are available to address it fully?

These are often decisions that should be made with and by school system leadership and, depending, on the nature of the risk, with counsel.

Once the plan has been approved, separate project roadmaps can be created and assigned to each applicable team to manage. Before embarking on that work, however, connect with each team to establish a reasonable schedule and a plan for keeping accountable to the roadmap. Create a time line of check-in points for each team to report back on their work, confirming that they are on track or reporting roadblocks, new resources needed, or other delays that will require adjusting the target dates.

This accountability is all part of the remediation process. A plan to mitigate and address gaps is useful only if it is all eventually implemented. Awareness of problems with the mitigation plan provides an opportunity to address them. Otherwise, those simply become gaps to be discovered in the future, and when it comes to impact assessments, the only thing worse than a known gap is an unknown gap. Be sure there is visibility on the progress of the remediation plan so that course corrections can be made when things do not unfold entirely as planned.

Chapter 13

Policy Development

It is tempting to think that compliance gaps could all be addressed by flipping a switch to restrict data access or by adding a line or two of code to correct a vulnerability. However, addressing gaps in data privacy compliance efforts often leans heavily on policy, process, and training. After all, things often go wrong in the first place because of a lack of rules, knowledge, and requirements for behavior. If people know what is expected of them and how to protect the privacy of student data, they are less likely to go down a path that creates risk.

A key part of the project roadmap to mitigate compliance gaps is ensuring that while you are addressing the issues, the same mistakes are not being repeated. For example, while you are revoking employee access privileges to data for which they have no legitimate educational interest, you don't want the same practices that allowed widespread access to data to continue, or you will end up back where you began. As you embark on a cycle of repeating privacy impact assessments over the years, one sure sign of failure is coming up with the same gaps, over and over, caught in a cycle of identifying an issue, mitigating it, and then ending up identifying the same issue the next time you conduct an assessment.

In addition, during the impact assessment, new compliance requirements were identified. You are now armed with goals to hit. It will take documented, enforceable policies and processes to truly establish the compliance program.

Creating Policy

Creating policy is a mixture of art and science. It is not simply words on paper. It is meant to be a guide for achieving certain goals and requirements. It should address both key concepts, which should be able to stand the test of time, and specific expectations, which may need to be adjusted as the ecosystem evolves.

For significant student data privacy compliance matters, leadership is responsible for crafting the policy. However, just because something is handed down from leadership doesn't mean it is going to be implemented effectively. To be effective, policy must be

- realistic;
- clearly defined;
- monitored and enforceable; and
- understood by the teams responsible for implementation.

Realistic policies are achievable and address specific concerns or requirements that are clearly defined and understood. Policy with no foundation, or with a foundation that is not understood, quickly becomes meaningless.

Resources also need to be available to implement a policy. For example, if the policy is that all employee laptops are to be stored in secure locations when they are not in use, those locations, be they cabinets, carts, or desk drawers with working locks, must be provided and available to each employee.

Policies need to be designed to support specific compliance goals, with defined objectives. Otherwise, processes and procedures can't be designed to meet expectations, so goals are never accomplished. Policy for which there is a clear rationale and an objective provides the context that allows development of processes and procedures that meet or exceed the goals.

Policy without an enforcement mechanism is also just words on paper. It may be implemented for a time, but how will you know that it is adhered to wherever and whenever it applies, in a consistent manner that achieves the desired goal? Policies need to include a mechanism for monitoring and enforcement, as well as an individual or team responsible for that work. Repercussions need to be in place to ensure that individuals who are expected to follow each policy can be held accountable.

However, before policies can be enforced, they need to be clearly understood by the teams responsible for following them. Don't assume that everyone in the school system understands that they have a role to play in protecting the privacy of student data, and what that role may be. Dissemination of policies needs to be accompanied by education. Ideally, the intent of each policy will be clear. However, the rationale behind the policy may not always be obvious to all stakeholders, and it is the rationale or intent that informs development of appropriate processes to implement the policy.

For example, a policy that explains that all requests received by teachers from parents to review and request to amend their child's education record need to filter through the principal's office seems clear on the surface. But why is it important? The reason might be that the school wants to ensure that all such requests for parents to take advantage of their rights under FERPA are managed by a central office where they can be recorded properly, steps can be taken to ensure that they are responded to in the proper time frame, and that all of the necessary information is provided to the parent.

However, if the teacher is not made aware of that, they may not realize that complying with the policy is important, time-sensitive, and necessary. It may be impractical to extract the entire text of FERPA and insert it into the policy as the rationale, and even if it were there, it is unlikely that it would be widely read. Instead, explain the intent of each policy in plain language within the policy, and provide the legal excerpt only as a reference. Provide training to arm the teams with the information they need to understand the impetus and importance of the policy, as well as their role in the larger compliance effort.

Crafting Policy

Policies need to be crafted before they are written. Establish what area of compliance needs to be addressed and the foundational concept for what you hope to achieve. A common one is "comply with FERPA." However, the law includes a variety of requirements, and it is *not* the policy. Giving people a copy of the law to read and telling them it is the school system's privacy policy does not tell how they are expected to behave in a way that achieves the goal of complying with FERPA.

Instead, take the law, or whatever area of policy you choose to start with, and break it up into its components. Then develop a framework for what compliance would look like. What needs to be done to meet the requirements of each part of the law? Give some thought to what behaviors are needed in order to achieve the compliance goal.

Once the basic framework has been identified, decide who will be responsible for drafting the policy. Will that be done by an individual who reports back to leadership with a draft policy, which will then be shared with the team responsible for implementing it for their feedback? Will a multistakeholder team that includes school system leadership and leadership of the group that will be responsible for implementing and enforcing the policy draft the policy together? Will policy be written by counsel or a compliance expert in collaboration with the school system?

How you choose to get the policy written may depend on the culture of the school system, the available resources, and what issue the policy addresses. Choose the path that is appropriate for your school system, taking into consideration available resources, expertise, and what is achievable.

WRITING THE POLICY

Often the biggest hurdle is simply putting pen to paper. The easiest way to get through that is to start with the basics:

- Assign a name and a number. It won't be the only one you write and it will be easier to identify, locate, and refer to in the future if it has both a name and a number.
- Write the goal. What is the policy meant to achieve? Why is it in place?
- What is the purpose? How does the policy connect to the school system's broader mission?
- Include relevant references. Is the policy an adjunct to an existing policy? Is it a mandate from school system leadership? Is it intended to address compliance with one aspect of a law? If so, note what that foundational material may be.
- Where and to whom does it apply? Who needs to comply?
- Who enforces the policy? Which individual manages implementation and enforcement of the policy? How are they authorized to do so? Who do people go to with questions about the policy?

- How is it enforced? What are the repercussions for not complying with the policy? Is it a condition of employment? Does not complying result in mandatory additional training or supervision?
- Are there elements of the policy that vary depending on context? If so, who is authorized to make those decisions? Who can authorize an exception to the policy, under what circumstances, and how are exceptions documented?

It cannot be emphasized enough that the policies are not restatements of the laws. The laws, along with district requirements, community norms and expectations, the school system mission and vision, and the ethical framework are combined to create the goals the school system must meet. Policies explain what is expected in order to reach those goals, and procedures explain what needs to be done and how it needs to be done in order to comply with the policy.

Be as cohesive and as comprehensive as possible. Think of your policies as "everything employees need to know to handle student personal properly."

As you write the body of each policy, be mindful of the language that you use. Are there elements of the policy that "must" be accomplished or that "should" be accomplished? If there are options, be clear about what those are and when they apply. If there are not options, be careful to avoid suggesting that there are.

Develop the Procedure

Whether or not the policy was not crafted in conjunction with the team that will be responsible for implementing it and following it, the procedure should be. The reason for this is that procedure is most effective when it is organic to the team responsible for following it.

Imagine that you have been performing your role in the same way for years, and one day your leadership decides that you have a new goal to accomplish, and doing so means changing the fundamental way in which you operate. Now imagine that you had no voice in how that happened, or in what the new operation needs to look like. Undoubtedly, you would find it disruptive and possible upsetting. It may spark a good deal of questions and frustration, and that may hinder your overall job performance and effectiveness.

Instead, create a procedure in collaboration with the teams that will need to follow it. Identify key stakeholders who will represent the impacted teams. If it hasn't already happened, take the time to explain why the new policy is being put into place, as well as the goals and requirements. Let them know that your goal is to work with them to develop a procedure to implement the policy, and to ensure that the procedure is as organic as possible to the way they currently operate.

You may choose to then develop a procedure and an implementation plan as a group, or you may provide some skeleton frameworks for what a procedure and implementation would look like for them to react to. Either way, this is fundamental leadership and change management process. It is about driving change to meet a goal. It is, by its very nature, often disruptive. It can be met with the classic symptoms of shock, anger, disorientation, anxiety, loss, and frustration. Change is often the business equivalent of grief,[1] and it is a very real phenomenon.

Managing organizational change requires care, thoughtfulness, advance planning, and methodical implementation. It is bigger than drafting procedure on a piece of paper. It is about asking people to learn, stretch, grow, and change in accordance with requirements that may wholly disrupt their idea of how they work. In some cases, depending on the existence or maturity of the student data privacy compliance program, it may be about changing the entire organizational culture. This type of transformational change requires asking people to not just change their behavior, but also their values and assumptions about their role in the school system.

It's why stakeholder involvement is critical in developing procedure. Asking people to change comes with repercussions. Those can be intense or minimal, depending on how well you manage it. Regardless of the size and scope of the change, it's helpful to socialize the change with key stakeholders before dropping a new policy and procedure on the teams. By working with the stakeholders who will be directly impacted, you are communicating that

- they are important, and their role in implementing the policy through a new procedure is important to the school system;
- their expertise in how the procedure can be most effectively implemented is valued;

- they have a critical role to play in protecting the privacy of student data; and
- their voice needs to be heard.

It is, of course, entirely possible that the team will come up with ideas that will not be tenable or sufficient to achieve the policy goals. Someone needs to guide, steer, and ensure that the procedure meets the needs. Everyone may not be happy with the final result, but achieving understanding for the need, being respectful of the input you receive, and incorporating the feedback into the procedure as much as possible will help to ensure that the policy goals are met.

The intended result of this work is that the teams involved in developing the procedure have a sense of ownership around it. That drives more adherence and more comprehensive compliance.

The procedure itself should be specific. While the policy explains what is expected in order to accomplish a goal, the procedure details what people must do to comply. For example, a policy might address a requirement that individuals not obtain access to sensitive student personal information unless they have a legitimate educational interest in the data and a need to have the access in order to perform in their role.

A procedure might explain how requests for access to sensitive student personal information are to be made and to whom. It might be accompanied by a form that needs to be filled out explaining the need for access, where that form will be submitted, and when and how a response will be provided.

A second procedure might be created for those who are responsible for approving such access requests. It could include specific requirements that must be met in order to approve the requests; how those requirements are to be assessed and the thresholds that need to be met in order to find them acceptable; how such requests, whether approved or denied, are to be recorded; and how and when access controls are to be revoked.

Not every procedure has to include a level of granularity that details each move. However, most procedures have enough detail that the expectations for behavior necessary to achieve the policy goal are clear.

As with policies, procedural documents should have an owner, that is, an individual responsible for implementation, monitoring, and enforcement. This is often the individual who can manage questions about the procedure and provide training or additional explanations about the requirements.

Policy and Procedure Subject Matter

A school system with a mature data privacy compliance program will usually have a fairly substantial book of policies on hand. It takes time, sometimes years, to build up all of the necessary policies. Start with the one that you believe will either be the easiest to write, perhaps because it illustrates a relatively simple behavior or applies to only a small group of employees, or start with the one that is aligned with what you have identified as your biggest area of risk.

The idea is to simply begin flexing your policy and procedure development muscles. The first effort may not be perfect, but it'll help build momentum. With consistent attention to addressing the needs of your growing compliance program, you'll see that a series of small accomplishments build up to big wins over time.

Here are some, but not all, of the policies and procedures you may need to develop for what will eventually be a more holistic data governance guidebook:

- data access roles and permissions;
- data classification;
- data retention schedules;
- data deletion and purging protocols;
- providing annual required notices to parents and eligible students;
- responding to parent and eligible student requests for data access;
- acceptable or responsible use policies;
- managing directory information opt-out requests;
- physical, technical, and administrative security safeguards for each category of data;
- administrative management of student records;
- classroom management of student records;
- technology development;
- website development;
- technology use;
- social media use;
- device management;
- disaster recovery;

- incident response procedure;
- technology acquisition requests;
- procurement;
- classroom technologies;
- training requirements and schedules; and/or
- communications.

Implementation

Although you may have worked collaboratively with the relevant stakeholders to develop the policies and procedures, the work is not complete until the materials are delivered effectively. That means they need to be accompanied by training.

If the change management process has been handled well, the teams who will need to be trained will likely know that change is coming and will have a relatively good idea of what that change will be. This will have been communicated in a deliberate manner, at specific times and places so as to not spark panic or rumor, but instead to provide context, prepare them for what is to come, and provide reassurance about how it will or won't unduly disrupt their existing work and performance goals.

Training is an opportunity to explain to everyone on the teams what the new policy is, the accompanying procedure, why it's in place, what is expected, how compliance will be monitored and enforced, and who they can go to with questions. Training may be delivered by leadership, by the individual responsible for enforcement, or by a leader of the team for which the policy and procedure applies.

The important thing is that training is delivered in a manner that is engaging and

- conveys the seriousness of the policy and procedure;
- adequately conveys leadership support and expectations;
- provides the broader context for the material in relation to the overall school-system compliance goals;
- establishes the legal or other requirement that the material is intended to address;
- explains how implementation will rollout;

- details behavior expectations; and
- provides an opportunity for trainees to have their questions answered.

As your book of policies and procedures grows over time, also be sure that it is kept updated. Review each document on at least an annual basis. If something needs to change, be sure any changes are made with appropriate stakeholder engagement and are rolled out with any necessary training. Note the date when each policy or procedure has been reviewed and when it has been updated so that it is easy to maintain version control over current documents.

The work you do developing and implementing policies and processes will prove to be foundational for what is often the very challenging change management process involved when working with technology providers.

Chapter 14

Working with Technology Providers

This is the area that often results in the most confusion, frustration, and fear among school systems, parents, legislators, and, in some cases, technology providers. In fact, when it comes to student data privacy, nothing seems to strike more fear into the hearts and minds of school system officials than the question of how to manage partnering with technology providers.

Before technology came into the classroom, protecting the privacy of student data didn't seem all that complicated. Even with the sometimes complex requirements of complying with FERPA and PPRA, there was a trust that the information was safe in the hands of the school system.

The truth is that there were likely few systems less secure than the locked file cabinets in an administrator's office, many of which could have probably been picked with a bobby pin. In those files sat a treasure trove of data, including Social Security numbers, parent financial information, grades, behavior, vaccinations, allergies, eyesight, hearing, sick days, physical fitness, interests, attitudes, aptitudes, eating habits, socialization skills, future plans, test scores, and more.

However, it sat within the walls of the school system, under their control, and that helped people feel comfortable. In addition, leveraging the data to identify how the student learned best, or to pinpoint when a student would benefit from additional support in order to stay on track, was an almost prohibitively time-intensive proposition, and sometimes simply impossible. It was a manual exercise in analyzing the data and looking for trends, and school systems didn't have the time or resources for that. That type of analysis simply wasn't possible at any scale.

Today, however, the fear around bringing technology into the classroom and protecting the privacy of student personal information is palpable. There is fear of FERPA, fear of technology, fear of technology providers, fear of marketing, fear of data and, mostly, fear of the unknown.

Luckily for school systems, the antidote to fear starts with knowledge.

START FRESH

Let's begin with a simple reality check: school systems are not meek and incapable of managing their ecosystem, and technology providers are not the big bad wolf, salivating at the prospect of taking advantage of a school system, looking for data to sell. It is a real fear that is simply not based on fact. Are there a handful of players on both sides who might fit that description? Perhaps, but they are few and far between.

How can we be so sure? After all, it is tempting to look at the billions of dollars being invested in education technology and equate that with an ulterior motive to profit off of the data of students. Undoubtedly, some naïve entrepreneurs have likely thought just that. They may have even received financial backing from equally naïve investors.

However, as with financial, health, and children's data, education data in the United States is heavily regulated. (Protections in the broader global market are robust across all types of personal information.) The cost of entry into the market can be significant. It may not be a long road to building an app or a website, but building a sustainable education technology business takes years, and the road to success is quite difficult. There is no viable or legal business model that involves selling or renting student personal information.

Many education technology providers earn revenue by selling or licensing their product to school systems, states, or through subscriptions. Some do accept advertising. Others shun that entirely. There are also often many small education technology developers that launch with no revenue model, just good intentions, fingers crossed and a dogged pursuit of foundation grants and investment to help get them off the ground. Some of these don't last long, while others find a maturity model and a path to sustainability. It often takes a lot of very lean years, caffeine, and passion.

Consider that for an education technology provider, the repercussions for causing a school system to fall out of compliance with FERPA mean that the school system is precluded from giving that technology provider access to student data for a period of five years. This is a news headline that would spread like wildfire. That provider would lose business from the school system and any number of other school systems across the country. It is a near, if not an entirely, business-ending proposition. Financial penalties for a technology provider under COPPA are currently $40,654 per violation, which translates to a per-student penalty.

It should be noted that the FTC, which enforces COPPA, is not in the business of putting companies out of business. Ultimately the total civil penalty depends on the severity of the violation, whether or not it was intentional, if the technology provider had violated COPPA in the past, how must personal information was collected, the sensitivity of the information and whether or not the personal information was disclosed, as well as the company revenue.

However, even with a small civil penalty, the FTC settlements are usually accompanied by consent decrees that include annual, independent auditing of compliance practices reporting to the FTC. Some of the consent decrees last as long as twenty years. That plus the legal fees of addressing a federal regulatory investigation can be devastating.

It also bears noting that companies are not legally allowed to send student personal information to a third party for marketing purposes without a parent or eligible student's prior permission, and depending on the type of marketing, it may be entirely precluded by some state laws.

Understandably, many schools and parents worry because they simply don't know what the technology is doing. It can be overwhelming to read through all those privacy policies, terms of use, and contracts and come up with the plain-English answer to the question, "What happens to the student data?"

Questions such as, "who has the data" and "where might it end up" are common, as are questions about whether or not data collected from or about students at very young ages will be used to prevent them from getting into college, getting a job, or otherwise closing off opportunities in the future. Some fear that technology companies are taking students' personal information and using it for financial gain by behaviorally marketing to students. Is that possible? Yes. However, remember that it is not legal under COPPA or most state laws, so there are serious repercussions if it does occur.

Is selling student personal information a common business model for education technology providers? No, and if the technology provider wasn't clear that was the practice before the data was collected, it would not be legal. If they were clear that was the practice, they wouldn't be in business. So it's a nonstarter. Selling student personal information is not a business model.

So, with that as background, let's presume for a moment that technology providers are interested in some of the same things you are interested in. That is, putting together a legal, beneficial, reasonable deal to bring technology into the classroom and support student success. How do you start to work with them?

Many school systems take an "us against them" approach when working with technology providers. It's a fear-based posture that often showcases a lack of real fluency or ability to articulate what it is that the school system reasonably requires. Instead, get educated. Empower your school system with the knowledge to meet the legal, ethical, district, and community requirements.

If you've done the assessment work and written the policies, you have your requirements in hand and are well on your way to having productive conversations with technology providers. When you know what you need, you are able to build business partnerships with technology providers that meet your data protection requirements and better serve the needs of your school system and the students and parents you serve.

A New Approach to Classroom Technologies

Of course, sometimes the school system isn't dealing with the technology provider because the technology came directly into the classroom and didn't go through an official procurement process. One of the most common complaints from school systems when it comes to managing student data privacy is that teachers bring free and low-cost technology products into the classroom at will. The products aren't reviewed in advance; there is no assessment of the privacy and security measures in place to protect student personal information. The school system doesn't really know how much technology is in the classrooms, and there is no oversight of who is sharing what data with technology providers.

Trying to intervene and establish a process of conducting due diligence on the apps and websites before teachers bring them into the classroom sometimes results in complaints that the school system is "stifling innovation." Attempts to assert a compliance structure or establish a process around bringing technology into the classroom are often perceived as disruptive and unnecessary.

Hit restart on these efforts. Establishing any new policy and process where there was none is disruptive. The roller coaster of change management is going to be present during these efforts. As a result, you have to plan accordingly. This will be fundamental culture change, so start slowly and build up not just your education around compliance responsibilities, but those of the teachers as well. You are in this together.

It Starts with Curriculum

A teacher wouldn't bring a book into the classroom without first reading it. More than that, they would read it, take notes, identify how assigning it to the students would help meet certain curriculum goals, build lesson plans around it, and more. The school library is not much different. At some point, each book in the library was read, and a determination was made that it was appropriate to give it space on a shelf.

Apps, websites, and other connected technologies are no different. The content needs to be reviewed to ensure it's appropriate and that it can help to fulfill a curriculum goal, and someone needs to determine how it will be utilized as part of a lesson plan. Start by encouraging your teachers to think about classroom technology products the way they think about books. You don't just read the cover and introduction and assign it to students. Someone does the work to go through it in detail to establish the educational benefit and how it will fit in with the larger lesson plans and curriculum goals.

Reaching Beyond Curriculum

Of course, when it comes to classroom technologies, one needs to assess more than just the appropriateness and educational benefit of the content. Privacy and security of the data matter.

As previously noted, school systems have legal and ethical responsibilities to protect students in their care. Today, that extends to protecting the privacy of their personal information in the education record, wherever it may be. Protecting the privacy of the personal information is protecting the privacy of the person.

The extension of that protection is control. Recall that, to put it in the terms of the law, FERPA requires that school systems maintain "direct control" over the use and maintenance of education records. A school system cannot hope to meet its legal and ethical obligations without conducting appropriate due diligence on the technology brought into the classroom.

BUILD A REVIEW PROGRAM

If you've determined that a classroom technology has educational value and a role to play in meeting the school system curriculum requirements, attention can turn to reviewing the data privacy and security practices of the product or service. Each school system has to review the technology it brings into its buildings, just as it reviews books and other curriculum materials. No one can tell you that a piece of technology complies with the laws, and implementation and interpretation of compliance in this arena belongs to each school system.

It may be tempting to look at what a neighboring district has reviewed and simply use those products, or to take something that a third party has deemed to be okay and skip your own assessments. The problem is that no one else's assessment has the answers for your school system. No one knows your policies, community expectations, or even the way your school system attorney interprets the laws or will defend you. Compliance is your responsibility. There's nothing wrong with leveraging work done by others to help get you started, but ultimately the decision is yours. You need to learn how to "read" technology.

Conducting a privacy and security review of each piece of technology before it comes into the classroom takes time, energy, and commitment, just as it does to read books. It also takes a certain level of expertise and advance planning. You need to know your data protection requirements, the technology provider's data protection practices, and the delta between them.

As with the rest of the compliance program, building a technology review program requires leadership and resources. Someone needs to be designated with the responsibility for building, implementing, and maintaining the assessment program. This individual or team needs to be provided with the training, resources, and staff to do the job well. This could be your chief privacy or chief compliance officer in conjunction with your chief security officer, chief information officer, or chief technology officer, or a combination of those team members. Discuss this with stakeholders before assigning the work.

Conduct discovery around the requirements and staff the team correctly, with adequate education, training, and resources to do the work. This is a big task and it is complex. It requires far more than technology expertise. It requires experience working through policies, reading and understanding contracts and legal requirements, developing business relationships, and negotiating agreements. Some of the work will likely be done in collaboration with legal counsel, but much of it may be done internally, and the team or individual managing this needs support and expertise to do the job well.

Start with Education

This is policy development, change management, and building school system capacity for owning the responsibility that comes with allowing technology into the classroom, all at the same time. It may be useful to refer to the roller coaster of change management once again, and to look for every opportunity to avoid the steepest slopes.

To begin, assemble the stakeholder group. This could include teachers, curriculum specialists, the information technology team, privacy and security representatives, as well as procurement or other business specialists. Introduce the problems revealed by the privacy impact assessment specific to third-party technology, the risks to the school system to bringing technologies into the classroom without a vetting process, and the risks and responsibilities individual teachers are taking on for the privacy and security of their students' personal information when they decide to use even a simple app in the classroom. Establish that you are not trying to stop their ability to use technology, but that you want to build a partnership to come up with a new and more responsible pathway.

If individuals have no context for change, they are more likely to resist it. If you provide the context, there is a better chance that they will understand and appreciate what needs to be accomplished. It may not make everyone happy, but there is a better chance that they will eventually adapt a more solutions-oriented posture if they understand their responsibility in the process. They will also be better positioned to contribute to developing a solution if they understand the intricacies of the requirements and the problem you are trying to solve.

Develop Policy and Process

In collaboration with your stakeholder group, decide on the policy for vetting technologies that are to be brought into the classroom. In the event that school system leadership has already established a policy in this area, start by working together instead to create the process. At minimum, the vetting process should include reviewing each product privacy policy and terms of use for alignment with your school system requirements for data protection and control. This is discussed in greater detail in the upcoming section in "Assessments and Agreements."

Be specific in the process about how classroom technologies are to be submitted to the vetting team. Will the teachers be responsible for investigating the educational value and curriculum goals met by the technology, or are there curriculum specialists who will do that work? What information is needed in order to begin the vetting process, and who will be responsible for gathering it? Will technologies be approved or disapproved, or will there be the potential for conditional approval?

Conditional approval is often a useful category when technologies have age or content restrictions that implicate certain privacy laws. For example, a product that is not intended for use by children under the age of thirteen might be approved on the condition that it be used only in classrooms where all students are thirteen or older. A product intended to assist in delivering surveys involving sensitive information might require additional approval from administration, which may need to manage PPRA notices before the product is implemented.

When creating a conditional approval category, be specific about the conditions under which teachers may or may not use the technology. This will help to avoid confusion and errors in implementation.

In addition, establish a policy to address whether or not the school system will allow the use of vetted technologies intended for a general audience, as opposed to only allowing those that have been created with an education use in mind. General audience technologies are often not subject to state student data privacy laws. The technology providers may not even be aware that their products are being used in classrooms and they may or may not have appropriate data protections in place. That does not mean that the products are not compliant with the laws, but it will require thorough exploration in order to make that determination. That exploration should include determining whether or not the provider prohibits use of the technology by minors.

Assuming that use by minors is acceptable, each school system must determine if these technologies could be used, on the condition that they are approved via the vetting process, or if, perhaps, the complexity of general audience technology is beyond the scope of school system resources to assess, and so they will not be permitted. Either way, it is important to make an informed decision about use of general audience technologies in the classroom, with full appreciation for the fact that they are unlikely to have been designed with consideration for student data privacy laws.

On that same note, school systems also need to develop policies that address use of social media in classrooms, as well as what school system employees may and may not share about their students on social media. Most popular social media sites are not intended for users under the age of thirteen, and so those sites should not be permitted for use by young children.

Behavioral and other tracking may be incompatible or run of state student data privacy laws with older students; consideration should also be given to the likely lack of control over their education records. In addition, school system employees discussing students on social media may present FERPA issues, and posting photos of students on social media can unintentionally jeopardize both the privacy and the safety of students. If leadership has not developed policies in this area, work with your stakeholder group to propose rules that provide for appropriate use and adequate protections.

Implement the Technology Vetting Program

Developing policies and procedures for vetting classroom technologies can be a fairly simple exercise compared with implementing the program. A significant challenge facing many school systems is that a large volume of apps, websites, and other connected technologies have been brought into the classroom by well-meaning teachers without having reviewed the privacy and security practices. Changing this means changing how teachers bring materials into the classroom. That can be disruptive, and lead to frustration and anger on the part of teachers.

There are two potential approaches. One is to "rip off the bandage," whereby you pick a date, at which time all technologies currently used in the classrooms that have not been vetted must stop until vetting has been completed. Approved technologies will be cleared for use in the classroom on a rolling basis.

The other approach is to permit continued use of technologies currently used in the classroom while they are simultaneously being vetted. Approved technologies will be cleared for use in the classroom on a rolling basis, and any technologies that are determined to be unacceptable will be removed from the classroom at that time as well.

The first method has the potential to cause considerable disruption in the classrooms. However, the process you choose will likely depend as much on the school system culture as it does on the risk tolerance and results of the privacy impact assessment. Needless to say, given the potential for disruption and backlash with the first method, the second method is the more commonly taken pathway. However, it is a risk-based decision that every school system needs to make for itself.

Since the first option requires little to no explanation, we'll focus on the second option. The idea here is, provided that school system leadership is comfortable accepting ongoing risk for a period of time, to begin a program of vetting classroom technologies. Under this framework, technologies are not removed from the classroom unless they are vetted and found to be unacceptable.

Start by taking the list of technologies used in the classroom that was produced during the privacy impact assessment. Determine which products and services are used most widely across the school system. Those are the products that should be vetted first.

Level-set expectations by communicating to the stakeholders the number of existing products that can be vetted per month.

As the products are reviewed, disseminate information about the approval status to teachers. Ideally, house this information on a web portal or other centralized, easily accessible location. This streamlines communication, builds transparency, and ensures that everyone has the same information at the same time.

Slowly, over time, you will build up a library of vetted technologies that teachers can pull from.

In the meantime, as you build the library, consider how you will manage requests to bring new products into the classroom. Will you allow that to continue? Do you have the bandwidth to review a certain number of new products while you continue to work on the backlog?

If the volume seems prohibitive, there are steps you can take to mitigate risk in the interim. One possibility is to train teachers to conduct some of the vetting. If you go this route, build a mechanism to ensure that there is consistency in the review process across all teachers. Arm them with information about how to read a privacy policy and terms of use, and provide them with a checklist of specific elements to look for. The checklist may include the required age of the user, what data must be shared, what happens to the data when the product is no longer being used in the classroom, confirmation that no sensitive data will be shared, and other items that you deem to be important for a baseline review.

Be sure to inform them that privacy policies and terms of use are legal documents, and that by agreeing to them, they are signing contracts. (Whether or not they have any legal authority to sign contracts in your school system is an issue to consider as well. More on that below.)

For any teacher who has been trained and wants to continue to bring new technologies into the classroom while the vetting program is being built, require that they print a copy of any terms of use and privacy policy that they agree to, and date and sign it. Those documents, along with the checklist for each product, may then be filed with the vetting team.

It is by no means a perfect system. It certainly does not address the fact that teachers may not be authorized to be clicking to agree to those terms. However, it does help to build accountability and awareness of the responsibilities that come with bringing technology into the classroom. It also brings to life the message that the terms of use are a contract, and clicking on it has the same effect as signing it. Sometimes that is enough to build in a much-needed pause in the flood of classroom technologies being brought in the door by well-meaning teachers.

As this exercise is going on, continue to build the centralized school system technology vetting program.

Whichever path you take, eventually there will be a library of websites, apps, and other technology products available for teachers to choose from that have been vetted by the school system. At that point, it would be appropriate and less disruptive to require that all new products be vetted and approved before being brought into the classroom.

Each school system will need to determine the right time and method for implementing a program to conduct advance due diligence on classroom technologies. It is unfortunate that so many school systems have significant work to do to get on the right track in this area. However, it is also an opportunity to band together with colleagues in other school systems and learn from those who have already implemented vetting programs. By connecting with those that are well on the road to having mature compliance programs, you can learn from their experiences, avoid mistakes they may have made, and implement best practices from the start.

ASSESSMENTS AND AGREEMENTS

After conducting a privacy impact assessment, you should have come away with fundamental requirements informing how you will manage student personal information in compliance with the laws, district rules, community norms and expectations, and your school system's mission, vision, and ethical frameworks. That led to development of policies that inform, among other things, what types of data you will and won't share with technology providers based on the sensitivity of the data; who in the school system is authorized to access, use, and share what data; the categories of data you have on hand; and the physical, technical, and administrative requirements for protecting each category of data. Those serve as a starting point for assessing classroom technologies.

The depth of the assessment conducted will depend in large part on your expertise, experience, and resources. It may be a deep, rich assessment in which you are working through each product as if you are a user, aligning the practices with the technology provider's stated policies, conducting a technical security analysis to uncover the security protocols and third-party calls on the product, and dissecting the privacy policies and terms of service, use, or other contractual agreements.

If you have the expertise and the bandwidth to conduct a technical analysis of each technology provider product you bring onto your network, do so. If, however, you're like most school systems and have limited resources, start with policy review. As you learn more about the technical security protocols, you can add that to the advance due diligence that you conduct on classroom technologies.

At a minimum, you need to know

- the minimum required information each technology provider must collect in order to provide the product or service;
- if that information is collected from the student or teacher;
- how the technology provider uses the data;
- whether or not the technology provider discloses student personal information and if so, to whom and for what purposes;
- how the data is protected, including protections in place if the data is disclosed to other parties;
- how you can access, amend, and correct data that is part of the education record for your own purposes or in response to requests from parents and eligible students; and
- when it will be deleted.

The answers will vary by technology provider and product. Some products will require a significant amount of personal information to function, while others will require none or very little. The ways in which the data is protected may vary, depending on the sensitivity of the data being collected. Data may be shared with third-party service providers or it may not be. With some products, you may be able to access data that is part of the education record directly, while with other products, you will need to ask the technology provider to supply you with the information or provide assistance in granting you access to the data. The products are unique, and there is no one-size-fits-all answer to any of the questions. However, you should have a good idea of how the provider operates in compliance with all applicable laws.

One important consideration then, is that the data privacy and security practices of each piece of technology are assessed in light of the applicable requirements you have developed for each category of data. For example, you may require that systems housing sensitive data be protected with two-factor authentication access credentials and that the data be encrypted in transit and at rest. That does not mean, however, that an app or website that collects no student personal information needs to implement those same protections. Blanket protection requirements simply won't scale. It's fine to go that route if you choose, but it will limit your technology options, often unnecessarily. What will scale is clear expectations and requirements for each category of data, when those expectations are based on reasonable industry standard practices.

Reading a Privacy Policy

With the assessment team in place, the educational benefit for the technology established, and required criteria on hand, it's time to start reviewing the privacy policy. The privacy policy is a legal document that explains what personal information the technology provider collects and how it manages that information. Technology providers are often criticized for having privacy policies that are long, complicated, filled with jargon, and hard to understand. Sometimes, that is all true. Some of them have improved over the years and become a bit easier to understand, as technology providers make more of an effort to make them easy to read. Some have even become downright monosyllabic in the drafting, with a light tone intended to convey enjoyment and ease of reading.

The laws require clear disclosure, and technology providers are beholden to those laws. Privacy policies must clearly and accurately reflect the personal information collected, how it is used, handled, and disclosed. However, not every privacy policy will be easy to read, and the light, breezy style is not always appropriate. It will also be impossible for every attorney to agree on what is "clear," what format is best, and what language is most appropriate. Again, one-size-fits-all does not apply in the business of school systems or technology providers.

There are requirements related to disclosure of third parties, tracking technologies, marketing, and other legal business that simply have to be there. There is regulatory scrutiny on privacy policies from different authorities, and as a legal document, it has to be appropriate and defensible in accordance with direction from counsel. Sometimes that will result in something that is easy to read and other times it may be quite complex.

However, if you read enough of them, you will find that they generally follow a similar format. Privacy policies explain what personal information is collected, how it is collected, what that information is used for, to whom it may be disclosed, how it is secured, how you may access it, whether or not there are third parties with access to the data and what they do, and when the personal information is deleted. Each policy should be dated to indicate when it was last updated and explain what options are available to review, change, or delete your information. It should also explain how you will know if the privacy policy changes, and what happens to the personal information if the company is sold, goes bankrupt, or undergoes some other business change.

There's more, but these broad strokes will get you started.

Take a look at the results of the survey of apps and websites that you conducted during the privacy impact assessment and pull together a sampling of privacy policies. Start reading. If the first one you pick up is incomprehensible from the start, try another one. Keep going until you find one that seems friendly enough, and you can get through the first few paragraphs without much trouble. That's the one to learn on. Keep going until the end, making notes along the way. Notice where in the policy you learn what products it applies to, and how the technology provider explains what they do with data.

If you find an app or a website being used in the classroom that does not have a privacy policy, the product should be removed from the classroom. Don't even bother vetting it any further.

If all else fails, start with the privacy policy on your school system website. (If there isn't one, add that to your gap report!) This one should be familiar enough that you can get through it, and if not, you will hopefully be able to easily track down the person who wrote it and have him or her provide you with a tutorial. If it's still too difficult to understand, imagine how the parents in your community must feel! Add "redraft website privacy policy to make it easier to understand" to your gap report action items.

The point, aside from identifying whether or not your own school system website privacy policy exists or needs work, is that once you get through one, you will find that more often than not there is a similar structure to privacy policies. The information is different in each, but hopefully you will gain a general sense of where to find what information in each policy. They may not all be entirely clear, but some of them will be and that is something to build on.

When you have finished reading a privacy policy, you should be able to identify what personal information the technology provider collects, as well as how and when the information is collected, used, secured, disclosed and deleted. You should know if the technology provider collects personal information from students under the age of thirteen, and whether or not the provider obtains parental consent for collection of that information directly or relies on the school system to manage those parental consents, how you may access and update student personal information, and if any tracking technologies are used in the product and for what purpose.

You should also know how you will receive notice if the provider makes changes to the privacy policy in the future. Note that nonmaterial changes require notice, but material changes require notice and consent.

The privacy policy should also include contact information in the event that anyone has questions about the policy. If you do have questions, ask! Behind that email alias is just a person whose job it is to help users understand the company's privacy practices. Better to start a dialogue and learn more about the privacy policy than to remain in the dark. This can be especially helpful if you're having trouble understanding the privacy policy in the first place. What you learn from that exchange may prove to be informative when reading other policies in the future. It may also tell you something about that technology provider's customer support.

Reading a Contract or Terms of Use

The privacy policy explains what personal information the technology provider collects and how that data is managed. The contract or terms of use is the document in which each party establishes its expectations and requirements of the other party. Whether it is a written document or a click-wrap agreement—that is, a statement that appears online and is agreed to via a click of the mouse—it is a legally binding agreement.

We don't often think of the click-wrap as a contract. They appear on all sorts of websites, apps, and other online services, and most of us are used to "clicking to agree" all across the Internet. It bears repeating that these are legally binding agreements.

When teachers bring apps and websites into the classroom, they are signing contracts with a click of the mouse. All of which begs the question of whether or not teachers in your school system are authorized to sign contracts binding your school system to an agreement with a technology provider. If the answer is "no," you have identified another gap, and a critical piece of information for discussion with teachers as you start to lay the groundwork for building a technology vetting program in the school system. Who in the school system is authorized to sign contracts, and how is that policy enforced? Once teachers know that these are legally binding agreements and understand all of the complex requirements in place for protecting student data privacy, some may be less inclined to take on the risk of clicking to agree.

The contract or terms of use is the business agreement between the school system, often on behalf of its employee and student users, and the technology provider. As with the privacy policy, start getting educated with one that you find easiest to read.

Content of the Contract

In cases in which you plan to designate the technology provider as a school official as the term is used in FERPA, and plan to provide that organization with student personal information under the school official exception of FERPA, you are required to maintain direct control over the technology provider with respect to his or her use and maintenance of education records. The contract is the key vehicle for establishing and maintaining that direct control.

As the legal document of control, it is important that it contain elements that establish the school system expectations and requirements for use and maintenance of education records. Whether you are working with counsel to write your own contract or using the technology provider's document or click-wrap agreement, consider the following questions regarding the minimum requirements for the agreement:

- What product or service is being provided under the agreement?
- When FERPA applies, under what justification in FERPA is the data being provided?
- What data will the technology provider receive, collect, or have access to?
- If personal information is being collected from children under thirteen, who is responsible for managing verifiable parental consent under COPPA?
- Is it clear that the school system maintains direct control over the use and maintenance of education records that the provider will receive, collect, or access?
- Is the educational purpose of access to the student personal information clear?
- Is it clear that the technology provider may not redisclose the student personal information except in compliance with FERPA and any other applicable laws or school system policies?
- Is the technology provider bound to maintain industry standard security protections for the data? Do they include restricting access to the personal information to only those who need the access in order to provide

the product or services? If the school system has specific data protection requirements for a data element that the technology provider will receive, are those requirements clear in the contract?

- What will happen to the student personal information when the contract ends? When will it be deleted?
- If it is a click-wrap agreement, and there is no stated end date, how can you request that the technology provider delete the student personal information and any student accounts when the product is no longer being used?
- How can you request access to review, amend, correct, or delete student personal information during the course of the contract, either on behalf of the school system or a parent or eligible student exercising their rights under FERPA?
- Has the technology provider agreed to provide you with the legally required notice in the event of a data breach involving your student personal information? Is the time frame in which the notification must be received clear? What are each party's responsibilities in the event that it is legally required to notify impacted parents and students?
- What verification method is in place to ensure that the technology provider continues to meet its obligations with respect to the student personal information? Will you request the rights to audit the technology provider's data privacy and security policies throughout the course of the agreement? Will you accept assurances that the provider undergoes third-party assessments as verification?
- If the technology provider is sold, goes bankrupt, or is involved in another, similar disposition of its business, will the student personal information remain protected in accordance with the existing contract and privacy policy?
- What is the procedure in the event that there is a regulatory agency or other legal subpoena for access to the school system information? When legally permissible, will those be referred to the school system, or will the technology provider need to notify the school system of such requests?
- Is it clear that the contract may not be changed without mutual written agreement?
- Who is liable for what?

State Law Requirements

A variety of state laws require that certain information be stated in the contract. One potential approach to complying with these regulations are to map the information in an existing agreement with the requirements of the state law. This maintains the integrity of the contract while ensuring that the state law requirements are contained within.

The more common approach is to write a contract addendum that lays out the requirements of the state law. Whichever approach you choose, be sure you understand what you are asking or what you are agreeing to.

Common Contract Pitfalls

Contracting requires working with competent legal counsel, versed in education law, student data privacy law, how the technology you are choosing to bring into the classroom operates, and the exchange you intend to facilitate. The contract you agree to needs to meet your requirements and be defensible by your counsel. Without all of that informing a contract draft, and sometimes even with it, the end result can be unworkable on one or both sides.

Here are a few common pitfalls that occur within school system agreements. These are just examples, aimed at supporting your drafting of stronger agreements in consultation with your counsel. (This by no means suggests that contracts provided by technology providers do not also have common pitfalls. However, this book is intended to support the school system with respect to its internal practices.)

- Not all technology providers, products, and services are alike, so there is no "one size fits all" agreement. Each school system has unique requirements and each technology provider has unique capabilities. Pay attention to the context for each agreement in order to make it the strongest possible, with consideration for the sensitivity of data shared and services provided.

- Insisting that a technology provider sign an agreement without making any changes often communicates that the school system is not capable of negotiating. If the agreement is not open for discussion, try to explain why in a cover note. Otherwise, not being open to any negotiation is sometimes a signal that the school system may not understand the agreement. In addition, since "one size doesn't fit all," it may come back to you with redlines anyway.

- Specify applicable laws, or ask counsel if requesting compliance with key student data privacy laws and "all other applicable laws" will suffice. It is not uncommon to see school system contracts that request compliance with a large list of laws or an entire state education code, many of which have no bearing on the technology provider, the student data being shared, or the business relationship at hand. It is again a signal that perhaps the school system is not knowledgeable.

- Accuracy is important. Misstating the laws, and even names of laws, happens frequently. Take the time to review the agreement to be sure the information is correct. Copying names of laws and lifting entire provisions from laws should be the easy part.

- It is unlikely that a technology provider will indemnify a school system for liability incurred for the school system's actions. The technology provider absolutely should take responsibility for its actions and its product or service. However, it's not terribly realistic to ask that the technology provider accept liability for actions, such as unauthorized access to student personal information, that result entirely from behavior stemming from the school system.

In addition, don't copy someone else's contract unless you know what it all means and are confident that it provides the protections that your school system requires. The contract used by a neighboring school district may or may not afford sufficient protections, meet the thresholds of your school system policies, or even be within the boundaries of how your counsel would interpret the laws.

Even if your school system uses the same counsel as another school system, the contract may not meet the school system policy requirements regarding use of data. Take the time to understand what you need, and be sure that you understand all provisions of the agreement before taking it on as your own.

Negotiating with Vendors

Nowhere is the fear of technology providers more apparent than in the reluctance to negotiate an agreement. This is not to suggest that negotiating is always easy and smooth. It is not. In addition, it is quite challenging to be faced with the prospect of negotiating agreements with all of the technology providers your school system may work with. No one on either side of the table has the resources to implement a smooth process for working through the sheer volume of agreements that come in and out of the doors.

However, one area that can hold school systems back from achieving strong, protective, appropriate agreements is the reluctance to negotiate. Redlines from a technology provider sometimes stop things in their tracks. Whether from lack of education about school system and legal requirements or lack of resources to engage, many school systems are struggling in this area.

There will be times when you find a technology provider's terms to be satisfactory, or vice versa, and agreements will be signed without comment. In addition, not everything will be subject to negotiation. However, often it is a required part of doing business.

With guidance from counsel, consider reframing the negotiating process. Redlines in a contract do not always mean "no." Instead, view redlines as the start of a conversation. It is simply one party saying, "This doesn't work for me. Can we try it another way instead?"

Ideally, each redline comes with an explanation, but even when it doesn't, it is an opportunity to try to find a mutually agreeable solution before having to walk away entirely.

By engaging in negotiations, you have an opportunity to build a stronger relationship with technology providers, clearly express your needs, learn more about how the technology providers conduct business, and give them a clearer understanding of what is important to your school system and what you expect of them in protecting your data.

Before engaging in a negotiation, you must know what it is that you can and cannot negotiate. For example, a tech provider may have no choice but to ensure that the contract is governed by the laws in your state. However, you may be able to be flexible on another point in the contract that does not minimize protections for your school system. Where can you be open to different language or pathways to compliance, given the type of product, the data that will be available to the technology provider, and the services that will be provided? What areas absolutely must be done in strict accordance with your terms?

Negotiating is not about winning and losing. If that is what you're after, reframe it. If that is what you think the technology provider is after, find another company. Negotiating is about finding a mutually beneficial resolution. When you can explain your rationale for needing language to be drafted in a certain way, you are enabling the other party to better understand your needs and perhaps come up with language that meets those needs in a way that is palatable to both parties.

When one side is uncomfortable with a line or a clause, it is often only when the other party explains why it was drafted that way that the goal becomes clear, and with it, the pathway to resolution. Without the dialogue, it is simply one side saying "yes" and the other saying "no." If neither knows why the other side wants something, there is nowhere to go to find a solution.

Negotiating an agreement doesn't always go smoothly, and there may be areas that simply can't be resolved. However, there is a good deal to be learned from negotiating, and when the deal is done, some groundwork should have been laid to build a stronger partnership with the technology provider.

Consider a scenario in which a technology provider redlines the school system agreement, and the school system responds by stating that nothing in the agreement can be changed. The technology provider is left with two choices: either sign an agreement that may put the provider at legal risk, or walk away. Perhaps that choice seems familiar from your side of the table as well. Neither option is palatable, nor does it kick off a constructive business relationship.

Now consider if the response from the school system had been to call the technology provider and explain what couldn't be changed and why. The technology provider now has context and may be more willing to work with school system counsel on something that is only slightly modified. At the least, both parties understand each other better. The technology provider has also demonstrated willingness to work with the school system, as opposed to walking away. (If a provider does walk away from an opportunity to partner without a conversation to try to resolve the issues first, you've learned a valuable lesson about how that provider conducts business before it got in the door.)

Reasonable, qualified counsel, knowledgeable in contract law and student data privacy laws can usually work through agreements. Power plays or "us versus them" mentalities on either side don't fix the problem. There is simply no substitute for knowledge and for doing the work.

No one wants to negotiate every agreement they engage in. The hope is that your school system has some well-drafted templates that it can customize for different types of technologies, and that you are educated or have competent counsel that can review technology provider agreements to ensure that they meet your requirements. However, there will be situations in which negotiation is required, and it is those times when digging in heels on either side of the table can be wholly unproductive.

In the end, be sure that your contract is legal, appropriately addresses the school system requirements, and that you understand it well enough to know where your boundaries are. Put yourself in a position to establish strong protections on student personal information in partnership with technology providers to better serve students and your school system needs.

Chapter 15

Training

As with many school system functions, no compliance program is complete without an education and training component. Almost every state requires that teachers engage in annual professional development programs. Some states require as many as 180 hours of professional development per year. Coursework varies widely. There is training on classroom management, social-emotional issues, bullying prevention, technology training, curriculum standards, academics, and safety issues, including handling blood-borne pathogens.

The one area that teachers and all other school employees are not regularly trained is in the privacy protection of student personal information, despite the fact that school employees handle student data every day.

In order to properly protect the privacy of student personal information, all school system employees must be trained on the issues. In fact, any organization where employees have access to personal information should be training in fundamental privacy protections. It is simply not responsible to not provide training and unreasonable to expect that a compliance program will be successful without accompanying education.

Of course, with so much training already required of teachers and other school system employees, the prospect of adding yet another training module to the pile can be daunting. In addition, it is hard to cut through the clutter of existing training to ensure that student data privacy training is impactful and relevant. There are also budget considerations, as building an adequate training program requires resources.

However, what if the only resources you needed were knowledge, time, creativity, and a platform on which to deliver the training? Would that change your appetite for implementing a training program?

Before we get to that, let's first consider what school system employees need to know about protecting the privacy of student data.

TRAINING CONTENT

All school system employees have a role to play in protecting the privacy of student personal information. Whether it is an administrator with access to all student records, an athletic coach with access to information about students' physical fitness and health conditions, a custodian observing altercations between students in the hallways, or a teacher managing student assessment scores, everyone has a responsibility to protect the privacy of student information. As such, training should be provided to everyone.

Often, organization-wide training begins with a standard, level-setting training. The idea is to teach everyone that they are a vested partner in helping achieve the school system goal to improve student-data privacy protections, and that protecting student data is an extension of their responsibility to maintain the safety and well-being of students in their care. It also lays the groundwork to prepare employees for future training. Information you choose to provide or discuss an initial training may include

- what the school system considers to be the positive uses for student data, and how the data may be used to further the mission and vision of the school;
- that the school system is subject to a variety of complex legal requirements to protect the privacy of students, further supported by district requirements and expectations from the community;
- basic federal and state legal requirements, how they have informed district policies, and where those policies can be found;
- leadership championing the importance of protecting student data privacy;

- that everyone has an important role to play in protecting the privacy of student personal information;
- where risk can be introduced through everyday behavior and how it can be avoided;
- how everyone can support the school system goals and requirements to protect the privacy of student data;
- basic data security training knowledge, including phishing awareness, password complexity, and how to securely send student personal information within the school system;
- that as role models, employee behavior with respect to student data privacy is part of how students learn about protecting their online privacy; and
- the individuals or teams that will lead the school system's creation or continued development of its data privacy compliance program.

Once everyone has received baseline awareness training, introduce customized training to each team. This can be developed in conjunction with team leadership, which should help ensure that the training is designed to be well received by the team. Content may include

- the basic legal requirements for protecting the privacy of student personal information, as the underpinning for school system policies;
- applicable school system policies and why they are important;
- expectations of behavior for the implementation of those policies, including procedures that need to be followed;
- technical or other team-specific training applicable to the group;
- how the policies will be implemented, enforced, and audited; and
- where employees can go with questions and concerns.

Training may be more or less elaborate depending on the existing level of knowledge, the maturity of your data-privacy compliance program, and the overall goals you have for the training.

Identifying accurate content is critical to developing the training. Thankfully there are a variety of qualified, free resources, including online training modules,[1] videos,[2] and webinars[3] from the US Department of Education and toolkits and one-sheets from the Consortium for School Networking.[4] Those are great places to start with building your training content.

In addition, check with other districts in your state. If they've already begun to develop their training programs, there may be opportunities to pool resources and expand the available content across school systems.

How and How Often to Deliver Training

Unless you are a lawyer or a compliance professional, or you have a deep and abiding fascination with student data privacy requirements, the idea of participating in student data privacy training may not be terribly exciting. This may be especially true if you are a teacher and student data privacy training is just part of the mountain of training you participate in every year.

Student data privacy training should be delivered at least annually. However, considering that it may not be part of the existing professional development, it may be difficult to introduce it to an already full schedule of training.

This is an obvious challenge but also an opportunity.

Training is sometimes best absorbed when it is dynamic. It doesn't have to be a "one and done" module. Instead, consider trying combinations of modules delivered in different ways, at different times to keep student data privacy top of mind in the school system.

For example, you may consider a baseline, level-set training that is a standard, required module delivered annually. Deliver team-specific, in-person sessions if a learning management system is not available, or use a combination of online modules and in-person sessions. Post required policy readings online, and record acknowledgment via electronic signature. Accompany that with brief video recordings from school employees delivering their top tips for complying with the policy, or a reminder of where to go with questions.

A monthly email blast with a security tip or privacy reminder, along with a poster campaign with privacy and security tips appropriate for students and teachers can also help keep the information alive, especially if the materials are rotated often and not left up too long so as to get stale. Invite teachers to take some of the tips in the email blast and work on a poster campaign with their students.

Challenge school employees to come up with posters, videos, or other media messages to emphasize the student data privacy requirements. Allow the employees with a creative streak to showcase their abilities while delivering a serious message. As long as the content is accurate, the medium matters less. It can be effective and engaging, even if resources don't allow for a bigger training investment.

It is unfortunate that one needs to compete with other priorities to capture everyone's attention about student data privacy. It is also unfortunate that in the plethora of state student data privacy laws that have passed, few have included funding to train school systems, or even guidance on how to implement their laws.

However, that is the current state of affairs. The job now is to pick up the gauntlet and create compelling, lively, fun, or at least surprising training that engages while providing the right information to arm employees with the information they need to succeed.

Parent Training

Parents have a role to play in protecting the privacy of student data and a keen interest in steps the school system is taking to protect their children's personal information, so training should be available to them as well. Some of the resources used to support employee training may be informative for parents, and PTAC does offer information specifically designed for parents.

Infographics and other visually compelling materials can also bring the information to life and make it easier to digest for parents.

If resources permit, arrange for demonstrations of commonly used classroom technologies. There are times when concerns about technology are due to the unknown. Being able to see the materials firsthand sometimes makes the benefits and protections clearer than any stack of policies or video trainings could.

Arrange for hands-on sessions for parents to try out some of the technology products used in the classroom, and use the opportunity to explain

- why the products are used;
- why the school collects personal information;
- how that personal information benefits the students; and
- how the school system protects student data privacy.

Student Training

Students need to learn how their behavior with technology, what information they share, and the ways in which they share it can impact their privacy and safety and that of others. Wherever possible, build lessons about data privacy into existing classroom work with technologies. Integrating even small data privacy lessons into daily work can be helpful. Encourage teachers to make note of the existence of a technology provider's privacy policy while opening up the product in the classroom, or remind students to not share their passwords.

Teachers may already remind students to log off of shared devices before they leave the class or to ask before providing personal information on a website or app. Empower your teachers to be able to explain the "whys" behind it all, and even to discuss how they choose the technology they bring in.

Children of all ages model or are influenced by adult behavior. As such, teachers have some simple opportunities to impart good data privacy lessons every day. Ensure that teachers are armed with information about expected data privacy and security behaviors when operating technology in the classroom, such as securing their passwords and locking their computer when they step away from the room. Remind them that what they do is what their student learn.

If you can create more robust training or lesson plans around this, by all means do so. However, if you don't have a lot of time or resources on hand and are looking for a place to start, take advantage of the free, credible resources and a little creativity to build something meaningful for your school system.

Chapter 16

Audit

Since a compliance program is about mitigating risk, the work is never done. Instead, it is a cycle of

- ongoing education about how to protect the privacy of student personal information;
- assessing existing policies, practices, and technologies;
- identifying and correcting or mitigating gaps;
- updating policies and procedures as needed;
- training; and
- monitoring and measuring results by way of an auditing and accountability program.

Figure 16.1 illustrates some of the key elements in the cycle of compliance.

Auditing the program is the only way to assess whether or not the work is effective in achieving the stated policy goals and in making continuous reductions in risk over time. There are always new risks to contend with in the form of new technologies and new behaviors, as well as new laws to keep up with and evolving community expectations. The bar is always moving, and there are gaps that may never be wholly addressed. The idea then, is to strive for compliant, strong, reasonable protections, and to examine them with an eye toward ongoing improvement.

An audit program assesses compliance with policy and process and efficacy of the compliance program at large. It establishes new benchmarks over time, which informs creation of new goals and the appropriate metrics for

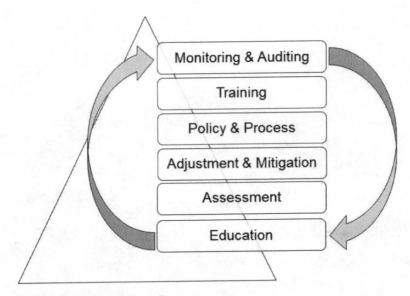

Figure 16.1   Key Pillars of Compliance

success. In turn, the success metrics need to be created in alignment with the
nature of each area of the program. For example, the effectiveness of a data-
security training program might be measured via volume of responses to ethical phishing campaigns before and after training. Volume of security
incidents and near-incidents may also be used as a measure of efficacy of
implemented security protocols.

Surveys of apps, websites, and other connected technologies brought into
the classroom, and the number of such products that are on the school system's approved list compared with the numbers not yet vetted might be a
measure of the efficiency of the vetting program and growing library or a
measure of compliance with the vetting program.

Auditing annually against defined metrics will provide insight into whether
or not the program is effective, and where aspects of the program might need
to be adjusted in order to meet the goals.

As part of any auditing process, data compliance policies should be
reviewed annually to ensure that they remain current in light of any regulatory changes, and to assess the need for any changes in light of other organization or technological changes within the school system. When changes are
identified, these need to be documented, and policies need to be updated

accordingly. Policy training also needs to be updated and implemented so that staff education remains current.

Procedures should also be reviewed annually and compared with actual practices. This can be determined through ongoing monitoring of practices, or though preassessment work including employee surveys or other instruments that will help to reveal discrepancies between the documented procedure and the behavior.

It is not unusual for procedures to be adjusted after implementation. It is only when they are implemented that individuals can assess whether or not they are truly effective and workable. However, monitoring helps to ensure that behaviors do not diverge so far from documented processes that they introduce risk or miss the goal.

As with policy updates, procedure adjustments should be made as needed, then documented and rolled out to the applicable teams with new training so that all impacted employees have a consistent understanding of expectations.

A privacy impact assessment should be conducted on an annual basis as well, as part of the auditing plan. The first one will be the most difficult. After that, if you are working against a gap-mitigation work plan, subsequent privacy impact assessments get easier. You can start with a series of preassessments to identify specific areas of risk that should be assessed, allowing you to narrow the scope of the actual assessment. This will also allow you to document whether or not the solutions and mitigation strategies have decreased risk and shed light on areas of the program and practices that still need improvement.

Hopefully, when the second time a privacy impact assessment is conducted, you will end up with a smaller gap report. However, since it is unlikely that all gaps will have been remedied after the first privacy impact assessment, the subsequent assessment helps to ensure that the school system remains aware of any existing concerns, and remains focused on and attentive to addressing all the gaps, not just the most critical ones that may have been addressed in the first year.

If it is not feasible to assess all of your policies, procedures, systems, and practices on an annual basis, develop a schedule of assessment to ensure that everything is attended to in a cycle of review. Ensure that all aspects of the data privacy compliance program are reviewed on a regular basis, even if you can't get to everything in the same year.

It is a cycle of continuous improvement, ever attended to, always fresh, and monitored for areas that can be improved to consistently build on practices to strengthen data protections.

Chapter 17

Parent Rights

No student data privacy compliance program is complete without a full appreciation of and respect for the rights of parents and eligible students to access, review, correct, and amend the personal information that they may have shared with an organization.

The rights afforded under the student data privacy laws are consistent with the concepts in FIPPS. However, the laws provide some degree of specificity regarding how those rights must be realized, starting with providing notice of those rights in the first place.

Looking at the laws again as the starting point, and not the ending point for compliance, consider the obligation to provide parents with information about their rights under FERPA and the procedures for exercising those rights. That information must be sent on an annual basis, and the notice must include that parents have the right to

- inspect and review their child's education record, and the procedure for doing so;
- request that the record be amended if they believe it contains information that is inaccurate misleading, or otherwise in violation of their child's privacy rights, and the procedure for doing so;
- consent to disclosures of their child's personal information in the education record unless an exception applies such that the law does not require consent; and to

- file a complaint with ED regarding any alleged failures by the school system to comply with FERPA, including with the obligations regarding the notice.

In addition, the notice must include the school system's criteria for determining what constitutes a "legitimate educational interest" in the student data, and what criteria the school system uses to determine who constitutes a school official.

Next, notice must be given to parents and students about directory information. This notice must include

- the types of student personally identifiable information that have been designated as directory information;
- the right of the parent or eligible student to refuse to allow some or all of that student information to be designated as directory information; and
- the deadline by which parents and eligible students must send their written notification to the school system opting the student out of the directory information disclosure.

There are other legally required notices under FERPA, including a requirement to alert parents if the school system forwards education records to other educational agencies or institutions in relation to a student's intention to enroll. Unless an exception applies, FERPA requires that school systems obtain prior written consent from the parent before disclosing education records. There are specific requirements for the consent, including that it must

- be signed and dated;
- specify what records may be disclosed;
- indicate the purpose for disclosing the records; and
- identify the party or types of parties that will receive the records.

Of course, all of that is just for FERPA. Recall that if you intend to conduct surveys, analyses, or similar activities in which you will be eliciting information from students about certain designated, sensitive topics, parent rights under PPRA will apply. In that case, with federal funding implicated, parents must be provided with advance notice of the surveys, and the school system must obtain parent permission before proceeding.

When federal funding is not implicated, at a minimum, parents must be provided with annual notice, at the beginning of the school year, explaining the intention to conduct surveys, any anticipated dates, and the opportunity to opt their child out of participating.

The notice needs to inform parents that they have the right to review the related instructional materials. Parents also need to be made aware, in advance, of any nonemergency, invasive physical exam or screening that is a condition of attendance, administered by the school, and not necessary to protect the immediate health and safety of any student.

If you have not yet developed policies to comply with all the conditions and requirements of PPRA, you must work with your parent community to collaborate on development of those policies.

Also consult your state laws, some of which may have additional notice requirements for parents. Almost all reiterate some of the existing parent rights under FERPA, but there are sometimes subtle differences in the requirements or expectations that need to be explored.

With respect to COPPA, inform parents about the technologies being used that will be collecting personal information from their child when the child is under the age of thirteen, what information or types of personal information will be collected, how the technology will support the educational purpose, how the technology provider protects the privacy and security of that personal information, and how consents are to be addressed.

It's not just the policies and notices that need to be done properly. If a parent does take advantage of their rights under any of the applicable laws, you need to have a process in place to respond. Under the laws, parent requests for access to their child's information are often time-sensitive. Prepare a process by which you will verify that the person making the request is the parent, compile all of the information requested, and respond. Some of the information needed may be stored by technology providers, so when contracting with those providers, ensure that the agreements address your need to access the data and confirm that they will provide that support to you within the required time frame.

It's a great deal of information for parents to sift through, and it may be challenging for them to place it all in the context of not just how the school system uses information for general administration but also how it connects to the technology program. Review the notices on an annual basis, before providing them to parents. Does they meet the legal requirements? Are they easy to understand? How do they help support transparency between your school system and the parents you support? Consider the language used as well as the length and comprehensiveness of the notice. Are they laden with legal jargon? If so, can they be rewritten to be more comprehensible and direct?

Also consider the context in which the notice is provided. For some parents, the packet of documents sent home at the start of their child's school year may be their first real introduction to you. Meeting the requirements of the law is obligatory, but how you communicate also matters. This is especially important as parents continue to have questions and concerns about technology programs in schools, with disclosure of personal information to technology providers often sitting at the top of that list. Many parents are not aware that they have any rights around their child's data privacy in schools. Does the way you provide notice help alleviate that problem?

You are the authority on the matter for them. The more you can connect with them, providing not just what is legally required but information about how it connects with your larger technology and student data privacy program, the more you will begin to earn their trust. At the very least, it will help you to open a constructive dialogue.

Chapter 18

Communications

Going beyond the legal requirements is key to building trust within your community. Legal requirements are obligatory. Parents want to see that there is more to the work you do to protect the privacy of their children's personal information than checking the boxes of the law.

How do you convey all of that to parents? What is the face that you put on the data privacy compliance program so that they can see it, understand it, and be confident in your capabilities and competencies?

Once you have established a data privacy compliance program, started to address the gaps, and created foundational policies and procedures for the school system, share your successes with parents.

If you've been building the data privacy compliance program properly and cohesively, you've already made parents aware of the efforts. They've been at the table in initial planning sessions for the function, provided feedback on their pressing concerns related to data privacy and technology, and understand how the school system envisions using data to fulfill its mission and vision.

That work must continue. As with developing training that keeps student data privacy responsibilities top of mind with employees, the same must be done for your school system parents. How will you keep the work that you're doing to protect their children fresh in their minds? What can you provide them with to demonstrate the progress you've made to improve your privacy practices?

A relatively simple first step is to dedicate space on the school system website to showcase the data privacy function, including the team, their qualifications and responsibilities, and perhaps any large-scale projects or improvements. At this point you will have also created a rather large packet of policies to govern the school system's data privacy practices. If you are able to make those publicly available, do so.

Try to keep your website content fresh. Include current policies, information about parent rights and how to exercise those rights, and importantly, how your use of technology and the student personal information supports their children and the school system's mission.

Keep the language on the website clear, simple, and free of jargon.

Give thought to how parents might better understand how you consider bringing technology into the classroom. How can you communicate the rigor with which you review those products? In addition, what are the ways that you can keep them appraised of what products are being used in their child's class, or at least across different grades or subjects? Have you explained why you use technology in the first place?

Empower teachers to be able to answer those questions as well. They are often the name and face of the school system for parents. They need to be able to explain what technology is used, why, how it benefits students, and how the student personal information is protected.

Also explain why data is collected. What is required by the state, and how do technology providers use the information they receive to benefit the students? If information is shared for research purposes, have the results or beneficial outcomes been shared with parents?

For many parents, sharing information about their child is personal, so they may be looking for results that have a personal benefit as well. As you tell a parent that information is shared for research purposes to improve the school system's graduation rates beginning in the next three years, is there a more immediate benefit to their child that can be shared? How does the school system's use of student personal information, tied to the school system mission and vision, benefit their child? Whenever possible, make it real for each parent. Try to communicate how the technology in the classroom specifically benefits their child.

Let parents know where to find the information, invite them to explore, and keep it updated. Communications need to be kept fresh. It conveys that you are paying attention and that you value your communication with parents.[1]

Chapter 19

Building Your External Support Team

It is challenging to consider creating any new school system function, let alone one that is as vast and complex as a student data privacy compliance program. It is no secret that many school systems do not have resources to find privacy counsel or the ongoing security and privacy leadership required to support the modern classroom.

However, there are some qualified, free, and low-cost resources, listed in the end notes, that can help, and there are also some simple steps that school systems can take to help build their strength around student data privacy.[1] Pooling resources between districts can be a helpful way to bring in education and training resources. In addition, don't discount the value of networking in your community. If there are companies in your area that collect sensitive personal information, such as financial or health data, they likely have robust privacy and security programs. It can be extremely informative to meet with their chief privacy and chief security officers. They will likely have valuable insights on building a compliance program and a good deal of experience to share. Meeting with them can also help you improve your understanding of industry standard practices for data protection.

Experienced professionals in other industries can support you on the fundamentals of data protection and may also be able to provide you with additional resources and contacts to consider.

Also consider reaching out to your trusted technology providers. As you build partnerships, there may be some that can provide you with thought leadership, not just about their product but about how they approach the function of protecting student data privacy and where they go to learn about the latest privacy and security developments.

Reach out to law firms that have data privacy practices. They will be connected to a whole network of qualified privacy attorneys, many of whom will specialize in education, and some of whom will be at the right price point for you. If you don't ask, no one will know you are looking. Do not underestimate the value and benefits of networking within and outside of the education sector.

Remember that there is no self-regulatory program or stamp of approval that can tell you that a technology provider's product is compliant with the laws or right for your school system. There is actually no true reassurance of that kind in any industry.

One tool in the toolbox to look at is the Student Data Privacy Pledge. This is a voluntary attestation by technology providers of certain practices to protect the privacy of student data. It can be a helpful starting point when looking for technology providers to bring into your school system. It is not a stamp of approval, nor is it inclusive of all the legal requirements. There is simply no such thing. However, it can be an element of support for your assessment and evaluation.[2]

Use your savvy. Be diligent and resourceful. The responsibility is yours. Be empowered by that to make your own decisions. Learn the facts, stay informed, and continue to build your program step by step. It takes time, but the more you know, the easier it gets and the stronger your program will become. Most importantly, stay true to your mission. That will be the lens through which you continue to make sensible decisions to protect the privacy of student personal information.

Conclusion

There is tremendous pressure for school systems to get it right when it comes to managing the privacy of their students. However, getting it right takes time, experience, and work. There is no quick fix, and no substitute for taking the time, learning, and doing the work. No industry has found a shortcut to protecting data privacy, and even well-resourced organizations don't get it right all the time. We cannot expect that the education sector will be different.

Managing student data privacy is a complex and often daunting proposition for school systems. Prioritizing care and education of students would seem to be more than enough responsibility to put on an organization, yet as a society, we expect more. Every day, school systems are expected to teach, feed, heal, care, supervise, entertain, and protect their students.

Administrative challenges and support services provided to students within school systems have become increasingly diverse in response to social and economic forces that create untold pressures on children today. Many seasoned business professionals would be put on edge at the prospect of managing just a handful of the services required of school systems in order to properly attend to the students.

Some school systems struggle just to ensure that parents have signed the proper forms so that the school system may document properly that, yes, dollars are needed so that children will have a meal that day. Others are challenged with issues of violence that have yet to be addressed well outside the walls of a school system, as well as a wide array of other mental, social, and emotional ails, plus the responsibilities of maintaining the physical infrastructure on a daily basis.

Yet despite those varied and critical responsibilities, resources are often stretched or lacking, and the complexities of managing it all keep growing with changing times. Still, we expect that schools will handle it all, educate the students, help them live up to their potential, and get them home safely at the end of the day. All the while, the pressure on the ecosystem around student data privacy continues to build in a way not seen across any other industry.

Somehow, some way, school systems manage to do it all. Not easily, and not perfectly, but the individuals who choose to spend their careers dedicated to lifting up the next generation make it happen day after day, year after year.

We need to approach the issue of protecting student data privacy with balance and reason from all sides. Legislators, community activists, parents, school systems, and technology providers need to appreciate that protecting student data privacy in the modern age is complex, new for many school systems, and that it is going to take some time to get it moving in the right direction.

There are no quick fixes, and the world is moving faster than ever. Students are growing up online, out loud, and school systems are keeping pace with new technologies, new methods, and ever-more individualized ways to ensure that no student falls through the cracks. There is a critical need for education to keep pace with the changing world. We cannot expect school systems to prepare students for the future without teaching them and empowering them to operate in that world, as it exists outside the walls of the classroom.

Technology is a necessary component of a best-in-class education. It is, by far, not the only component, and technology is not the teacher. However, students need to be able to work, learn, compete, play, and grow in ways that give them the greatest opportunities and greatest advantages to exceed even what their active imaginations can dream up. Technology is part of the world in which that is possible.

As responsible guides, protectors, and leaders, we need to ensure that students have all of that and more at their disposal, and we have to ensure that it is safe, age-appropriate, and empowering for them. It is no easy feat, and the responsibility never ends.

But if it's true that organizations are only as good as their people, then school systems are among the best in the world. Because despite the challenges, complexities, bureaucracies, politics, pressures, and pitfalls, the people who keep the doors open and show up every day always seem to find a way.

The challenge, then, is often not so much doing the work but not getting overwhelmed by all there is to be done, both on its own merits and in the face of other critical priorities.

The answer is to start where you are. Put it in perspective. Pull away from the noise and remember that the path to success is simply to start. Just learn and begin. Data privacy compliance is a function that grows incrementally over time. Do what you can for now and map out the plan you need to follow to get it right. Don't expect to get it all done in one day, one month, or even one year. Do expect that when you begin, small achievements will make a big impact.

Whether your school system is large or small, well-resourced or struggling to keep the doors open, there is always success to be found in taking the first step.

Keep your eyes off what you don't have in terms of resources, and stay focused on what you do have in terms of guidance, support, creativity, a school system mission to guide you, and hopefully now, a roadmap to put you on the right path to extending your duty of care for students to encompass their privacy.

Notes

INTRODUCTION

1. Arthur W. Foshay, "The Curriculum Matrix: Transcendence and Mathematics," *Journal of Curriculum and Supervision* 6, no. 4 (Summer 1991): 277–93, http://www. ascd.org/ASCD/pdf/journals/jcs/jcs_1991summer_foshay.pdf.

2. Monica Butler, Patrick McCormick, and Mikaela Pitcam, "The Legacy of InBloom," *Data and Society*, 2007, https://datasociety.net/pubs/ecl/InBloom_feb_2017.pdf.

CHAPTER 1

1. The Data Governance Institute. Definitions of Data Governance, http://www. datagovernance.com/adg_data_governance_definition/.

2. Danah Boyd, *It's Complicated* (New Haven: Yale University Press, 2014).

CHAPTER 2

1. Monica Butler, Patrick McCormick, and Mikaela Pitcam, "The Legacy of InBloom," *Data and Society*, 2017, https://datasociety.net/pubs/ecl/InBloom_feb_2017.pdf.

2. Natasha Singer, "Deciding Who Sees Student Data," illustration by Minh Uong, *New York Times*, October 5, 2013, http://www.nytimes.com/2013/10/06/business/deciding-who-sees-students-data.html.

3. Ibid. "Students are currently subject to more forms of tracking and monitoring than ever before," Khaliah Barnes, a lawyer at the Electronic Privacy Information Center in Washington who appeared via video conferencing, told the room packed with parents. "While we understand the value of data for promoting and evaluating personalized learning, there are too few safeguards for the amount of data collected and transmitted from schools to private companies."

4. Senator Edward J. Markey, 2013, https://www.markey.senate.gov/documents/2013-10-22_FERPA.pdf.

5. Secretary Arne Duncan, 2014, https://www.markey.senate.gov/documents/2014-01-10_Education_Privacy.pdf.

6. Joel Reidenberg, N. Cameron Russell, Jordan Kovnot, Thomas B. Norton, Ryan Cloutier, and Daniela Alvarado, "Privacy and Cloud Computing in Public Schools," *Center on Law and Information Policy*, Book 2, December 13, 2013, https://ir.lawnet.fordham.edu/clip/2/.

7. Ibid.

CHAPTER 3

1. "Family Educational Rights and Privacy Act," 20 U.S.C. § 1232g; 34 CFR Part 99.

2. US Department of Education Privacy Technical Assistance Center and the Family Policy Compliance Office, Protecting Student Privacy, https://studentprivacy.ed.gov/resources/data-de-identification-overview-basic-terms.

3. General Education Provisions Act, https://legcounsel.house.gov/Comps/General%20Education%20Provisions%20Act.pdf.

4. "Protection of Pupil Rights Amendment," 20 U.S.C. § 1232h (2000 and Supp. IV 2004), http://familypolicy.ed.gov/content/ppra-requirements.

5. Data Quality Campaign, Education Data Legislation Review: 2017 State Activity, https://dataqualitycampaign.org/resource/2017-education-data-legislation/.

6. Student Online Privacy Protection Act, https://leginfo.legislature.ca.gov/faces/billNavClient.xhtml?bill_id=201320140SB1177.

7. Ibid.

8. New York State Education Law Section 2D, http://public.leginfo.state.ny.us/lawssrch.cgi?NVLWO.

9. Louisiana R.S. 17:3913 and 3996(B)(34), http://www.legis.la.gov/legis/ViewDocument.aspx?d=916157.

10. 16 CFR Part 312, Children's Online Privacy Protection Rule, https://www.ecfr.gov/cgi-bin/text-idx?SID=4939e77c77a1a1a08c1cbf905fc4b409&node=16%3A1.0.1.3.36&rgn=div5.

11. Federal Trade Commission, "Comply with COPPA: Frequently Asked Questions," https://www.ftc.gov/tips-advice/business-center/guidance/complying-coppa-frequently-asked-questions#Schools.

12. Federal Trade Commission, "Comply with COPPA: Frequently Asked Questions," https://www.ftc.gov/tips-advice/business-center/guidance/complying-coppa-frequently-asked-questions#COPPA Enforcement.

13. Federal Communications Commission, "Children's Internet Protection Act Consumer Guide," https://www.fcc.gov/consumers/guides/childrens-internet-protection-act.

14. United States Department of Agriculture Food and Nutrition Service, National Student Lunch Act, https://www.fns.usda.gov/nslp/history_5.

15. US Department of Health and Human Services, US Department of Education, "Joint Guidance on the Application of the Family Educational Rights and Privacy Act (FERPA) and the Health Insurance Portability and Accountability Act of 1996 (HIPAA) to Student Health Records," November 2008, https://www2.ed.gov/policy/gen/guid/fpco/doc/ferpa-hipaa-guidance.pdf.

16. Ponemon Institute Research Report, "2017 Cost of a Data Breach Study," June 2017, Ponemon Institute.

17. Ibid.

18. US Department of Education Privacy Technical Assistance Center and the Family Policy Compliance Office, Protecting Student Privacy, Historic Findings Letters, https://studentprivacy.ed.gov/historic-findings-letters.

19. Federal Trade Commission, Legal Resources, https://www.ftc.gov/tips-advice/business-center/legal-resources?type=case&field_consumer_protection_topics_tid=246.

CHAPTER 5

1. US Department of Education Privacy Technical Assistance Center and the Family Policy Compliance Office, Protecting Student Privacy, "Letters of Importance," January 2018, https://studentprivacy.ed.gov/topic/letters-importance.

2. Ponemon Institute Research Report, "2017 Cost of a Data Breach Study," Ponemon Institute, June 2017.

3. DataBreaches.net; PrivacyRightsClearinghouse.org.

CHAPTER 6

1. US Department of Education Privacy Technical Assistance Center offers a variety of free education resources, as does the Consortium of School Networks (CoSN). CoSN also offers online privacy training.

2. Los Angeles Unified School District, https://achieve.lausd.net/about.

3. Chicago Public Schools, http://cps.edu/Pages/Students.aspx.

4. Lafayette Parish School System, https://www.lpssonline.com/site22.php.

5. Clark County School District, https://newsroom.ccsd.net/social-media/.

6. Broward County Public Schools, http://browardschools.com/.

7. Consortium for School Networking, http://www.cosn.org/Privacy; US Department of Education Privacy Technical Assistance Center and the Family Policy Compliance Office, Protecting Student Privacy, https://studentprivacy.ed.gov/.

CHAPTER 9

1. Federal Trade Commission, "Start with Security," https://www.ftc.gov/system/files/documents/plain-language/pdf0205-startwithsecurity.pdf; Information Systems Audit and Controls Association (ISACA), http://www.isaca.org/cobit/pages/default.aspx; International Organization for Standardization (ISO) https://www.iso.org/home.html; National Institute of Standards and Technology (NIST), https://www.nist.gov/; Open Web Application Security Project (OWASP), https://www.owasp.org/index.php/Main_Page.

2. Ibid.

CHAPTER 13

1. Stephen Warrilow, "Strategies for Managing Change," http://www.strategies-for-managing-change.com/kubler-ross.html.

CHAPTER 15

1. US Department of Education Privacy Technical Assistance Center and the Family Policy Compliance Office, Protecting Student Privacy, https://studentprivacy.ed.gov/content/online-training-modules.

2. US Department of Education Privacy Technical Assistance Center and the Family Policy Compliance Office, Protecting Student Privacy, https://studentprivacy. ed.gov/content/guidance-videos.

3. US Department of Education Privacy Technical Assistance Center and the Family Policy Compliance Office, Protecting Student Privacy, https://studentprivacy. ed.gov/content/recorded-webinars.

4. Consortium for School Networking, http://cosn.org/protectingprivacy.

CHAPTER 18

1. The Consortium for School Networking (CoSN) Trusted Learning Environment Program was designed in part to help school systems demonstrate and communicate specific steps they take to protect the privacy of student data, documented with evidence provided by each participating school system. The author is the project director for this program on behalf of CoSN.

CHAPTER 19

1. US Department of Education Privacy Technical Assistance Center provides school systems with information in the form of enforcement letters of note, guidance memos, videos, best practices, and training modules. Consortium for School Networking (CoSN) Privacy Initiative provides toolkits, infographics, training courses, online networking, clinics, and workshops for school system leaders and technology specialists, as well as the Trusted Learning Environment program. The author is the project director for the CoSN initiatives mentioned here.

2. Future of Privacy Forum, Software and Information Industry Association, "Student Privacy Pledge," https://studentprivacypledge.org/.

About the Author

Source: Lucas Noonan

Linnette Attai has been building organizational cultures of compliance and guiding clients through the complex obligations governing data privacy matters, user safety, and marketing for over twenty-five years. As founder of PlayWell, LLC, Linnette's primary focus is the education and entertainment sectors, where she works with private and public companies, schools and districts, trade organizations, lawmakers and policy influences. She serves as a virtual chief privacy officer and data protection officer to select clients, and speaks nationally on compliance matters. Learn more at PlayWell-LLC.com.